CHRISTMAS IN OLD SANTA FE

CHRISTMAS IN OLD SANTA FE

BY

Pedro Ribera Ortega

Illustrated by
Orlando Padilla

Sunstone Press
Santa Fe, New Mexico

SECOND EDITION

10 9 8 7 6 5 4

Printed in the United States of America

_____

Library of Congress Cataloging in Publication Data:

Ortega, Pedro Ribera.
        Christmas in old Santa Fe. Illustrated by Orlando Padilla.
        (2nd ed.) Santa Fe, NM, Sunstone Press, 1973.
        v, 102 p. Illus. 23 em.

        1. Christmas—New Mesxico—Santa Fe. I. Title.
GT4986.N6R52   1973   73-90581
ISBN: 0-913270-25-3   394.2'68282'0978956   MARC

_____

Published by   SUNSTONE PRESS
                    P.O. Box 2321 / 239 Johnson Street
                    Santa Fe, New Mexico 87504-2321 / USA
                    (505) 988-4418 / FAX (505) 988-1025 / orders 800-243-5644

Se dedica esta obra
a mis abuelos:
Don Román Ribera y Doña Catarina Sánchez
Don Ramón Ortega y Doña Sotera Gonzales

Del Verbo Divino

Del Verbo divino
La Virgen preñada
Viene de camino
¿Si le dais posada?
—San Juan de la Cruz
(1542-1591)

Concerning the Divine Word

With the divinest Word, the Virgin
Being pregnant, down the road
Comes walking; yes, you'll grant her
A room in your abode, won't you?
—St. John of the Cross

On Rereading
The Christmas Story

How like that manger is the human heart:
Plainly functional, yet shaped to hold,
In trust, the sacred rhythm of a life,
Deep-cradled from the darkness and the cold.

How like that stable is the human heart:
The brute emotions stamping at its doors,
Yet hallowed as the birthing-place of love,
And now without its kingly visitors.

—R. H. Grenville

CONTENTS

FOREWORD
PETER RIBERA ORTEGA and SANTA FE

Flanked by the Sangre de Cristo range and the storied Rio Grande, the ancient city of Santa Fe accepts her honors and accomplishments with Old World grace. A brace of adjectives scarcely hints at her color and illustrious past. A small city, her emanations cover the world. Ranging from her first distinction as North America's oldest Capital City, her prestige is compounded of a fascinating variety.

Celebrated as the western terminus of the Santa Fe Trail, her early days provide a brilliant splash, sometimes red with blood, in American history. Her tree shaded, adobe environment provided the springboard for General Lew Wallace to write his epic BEN-HUR. Her full name is: *La Villa Real de la Santa Fe de San Francisco de Asís* (The Royal City of the Holy Faith of St. Francis of Assisi). As Santa Fe it has become the trade-mark of our largest railway system. The scene of many Indian uprisings, she was the seat of operations for a pioneer apostolic man, Bishop Jean-Baptiste Lamy, the hero of Willa Cather's DEATH COMES FOR THE ARCHBISHOP. Demonstrating her continuous vitality, Santa Fe now enjoys an international reputation for the stature of her summer Opera seasons. Charming, unpredictable Santa Fe is a romantic off-beat jewel among our standardized American cities.

But hidden by the handsome Territorial style State Capitol, the gay Plaza, the venerable Palace of the Governors, the luxurious La Fonda Hotel, and the Cathedral of St. Francis, is an inner life, rooted in her heritage when Spain ruled her thoughts, streets and spaces. This Spanish ancestry accounts only in part for her character and special atmosphere, not of man's devising. There remains a curious and unexplained elation about this serene little city. Natives are a part of it, but visitors, even the most insensitive, respond. The present Archbishop, the most Reverend Edwin V. Byrne seems to have the answer. More than twenty-five priests and Franciscan brothers have been martyred in the hallowed surrounding countryside. Is this not responsible for the holy emanations which pervade this city of St. Francis of Assisi?

Steeped in the traditions and the history of Santa Fe, endowed by piety and temperament to express her inner life, Peter Ribera Ortega is a young man, modest and scholarly. The Ortegas are prominent in the list of the first arrivals in Santa Fe, three hundred and fifty years ago. Peter Ribera Ortega is a descendant of these pioneers.

Peter has a dedicated mission in writing this charming, historically correct account of customs, mores and celebrations. Many writers from other climes and lands, seduced by the surface charm of Santa Fe, have distorted many things sacred to the Catholic-Spanish Southwest. But the truth is far more interesting and colorful than the fiction so invented. Peter Ortega has therefore performed a service to Santa Fe and her traditions as well as to all lovers of the Southwest, by presenting the great living legends inspired by the truth. His keen mind reviews the past and his background provides the authority. He was educated in both the parochial and public schools of Santa Fe. His sense of historical awareness was developed by the beneficent influence of maternal grandparents. He early became conscious of the importance of Spanish Catholicism in day by day living. Fortunately he was taught to appreciate the value of an education in both Spanish and English. His formal education is in logical sequence. Matriculation at St. Mary's University in San Antonio, Texas, was followed by a Bachelor's degree from St. Michael's College in Santa Fe. Then came an invitation, from the manager of the NEW MEXICAN, to edit *El Nuevo Mexicano*. As editor of this Spanish weekly he had an opportunity to analyze the thoughts and politics not only of the southwestern United States, but also the countries of Latin America.

Supplementing his editorship, he continued his research into the life and times of the great Padre Martinez of Taos, plus the so-called "Mexican Period" and the "Americano Invasion" times and events. After three fruitful years as editor, he reacted to the lure of teaching experience by entering the faculty of the Santa Fe public schools. Here he taught Developmental and Remedial reading and Spanish on the Junior High level. He has now become assistant-director of the Spanish program on the Elementary level. And he has appropriate future plans! This is the formal outline. But the resultant mental and spiritual maturity of this young man is his great distinction. His thoughtfulness and devotion to his Faith and his friends are already a Santa Fe legend.

None of these activities have prevented him giving time and effort to projects close to his heart. He has been publicity director for *La Cofradía de La Conquistadora* since 1956, and has been *Presidente General* of the *Caballeros De Vargas*. Both projects overlap in promoting renewed interest in the spiritual and cultural hispanic background and heritage.

Americans unaware of their Spanish background have missed a rich experience and a cultural vitality of which we can be very proud. Art, music and architecture as well as Faith are the stronger in our country because of the soundness of the colorful past requeathed by our Spanish ancestors. A subject never properly stressed in our American history books.

In this delightful volume, Peter Ribera Ortega pleases and entertains us with the great truths of the past, ranging from the ever new and galvanizing story of *La Virgen de Guadalupe*, to the charm and rightness of a medieval mystery drama, *Los Pastores*. Each chapter is fascinating and the reader will experience an expanding understanding of the lively and beautiful events which form their fabric and background. A kind of gracious living not yet gone from this earth. Let there be a renaissance of those great, wholesome and colorful days!

Merle Armitage

PREFACE

Christmas is celebrated in different ways in different lands through religious observances and folk ways. In Santa Fe, sometimes called the City Different, Christmas celebrations are unique.

Uprooted from 16th century Europe, particularly Spain, when transplanted to the New World, such celebrations were adapted and transmuted. Coming up from the south over the old Chihuahua Trail into the Southwest with the soldiers of the King of Spain, the Franciscan Missionaries brought the traditional church observances. Those Spanish explorers and colonists who had tarried in Old Mexico absorbed some of the customs of that land, adding or mingling these with theirs from the Mother country. For several centuries, the *padres* and the *conquistadores* in their contacts with the Indians of this area still observed their native customs, although Indian pageantry and symbolism crept in here and there.

In the 17th century, just ten years after Oñate had founded the first capital of New Mexico, other colonists were arriving on the New England coast. The severe Pilgrim way of life contrasted vividly with the elaborate and even flamboyant Spanish mode of living. As the original colonies expanded and settlers hunted new lands, they pushed further and further Westward, and at the end of the old Santa Fe Trail, New England and New Spain met in New Mexico at Santa Fe.

Manufactured goods of many kinds came from the East, such as had not come up over the Chihuahua Trail (when parrot feathers were traded for New Mexico turquoise). Having more things to do with, it was only natural that certain modifications would be made in religious and other traditional celebrations; further items were added by the coming of the railroad in 1880 with its increased transportation facilities.

To the original ingredients of explorers and colonizers were added adventurers, health seekers and homesteaders coming to live in the land of the Pueblo Indians. A fusion of the

iv

mores and traditions of all of these has become Christmas in Santa Fe.

Several years ago near the holiday season I chanced to meet Peter Ortega in the Museum Library and mentioned to him that in trying to gather material for a story of Christmas customs, I had run into many contradictions by writers on the subject. This situation was well known to Peter Ortega, a keen student of New Mexico history, and he expressed to me, then, the hope that he might compile material about Christmas customs for a book.

Happily, he has done that in this volume "CHRISTMAS IN OLD SANTA FE," after much research into the origins of the customs and the process of their development into today's traditional observances. Peter Ortega, being a descendant of one of our old Spanish families, also has had his own experiences and family folklore to draw upon. Working closely with Orlando Padilla, a fellow member of *Caballeros de Vargas*, who has illustrated this authoritative book, the spirit of Christmas in Santa Fe has been sympathetically projected; something that visitor, newcomer, old resident and native born will take pleasure in reading, and in so doing heighten his personal enjoyment of Christmas time in Santa Fe.

Mary A. Comfort

CHAPTER 1

La Virgen de Guadalupe

Madonna of the Americas

The story is told that when *Santiago,* the apostle James the Greater, died and went to heaven, he asked God for a special favor. He asked that Spaniards should always be the handsomest and the wittiest people in the world. This request was granted. But then St. James went too far. He asked that Spain be granted good government as well, and the Lord, in punishment for such presumption, decreed that Spain and her many colonies would never have any government at all.

And one is inclined to believe the legend. In 1519 the great *conquistador* Hernán Cortés 'came, saw and conquered' Mexico, but the inordinate Spanish passion for individuality created confusion in the government of *la Nueva España.* So Divine Providence had to take over the situation. The apparitions and message of *Santa María de Guadalupe,* in 1531, on the rocky hill called Tepeyac provided the necessary spiritual foundation for Christian brotherhood in the Americas.

In Old Santa Fe and throughout the Southwest, the Christmas season might be said to begin with the traditional *fiesta de la Virgen de Guadalupe,* December 12th. And while it is not directly related to the details of the manger scene, it is the most natural invitation to prepare for the ever-new celebration of Christ's birthday. The centuries-old feastday of Our Lady of Guadalupe is the most important Marian festival in the Americas, as well it might be, for it is synonymous with Christianity in the New World! No more dramatic history can be found than the origin of this festivity. And Old Santa Fe makes sure it preserves this precious tapestry of indo-hispanic culture.

1

Luminarias, bonfires, burning brightly on the eve of the 12th of December around the local Guadalupe Church bring to mind the colorful and traditional decorations which Santa Feans associate with the joyous feast of Christmas. The pealing of the melodious Guadalupe bells on the eve of its patronal feastday, the symbolic red roses, and the happy crowds that fill to overflowing the ancient Marian Shrine, all denote the popularity of the historic devotion to *Santa María de Guadalupe,* Empress and Patroness of All the Americas.

New Mexico, having been for centuries an integral part of the world-wide and far-flung Spanish Empire, shares proudly the cultural conotation that surrounds the Feast of Guadalupe and the spiritual wisdom and beauty that it propounds.

We have but to place the story of the famous apparitions of the Virgin of Guadalupe, in 1531, in its historical perspective to comprehend, however briefly, the fascinating saga of the conquest and colonization of Columbus' New World. Not only the Iberian Motherland, the South American and Central Amereican republics, the lands of the Carribean and the faraway Philippines, but southwestern New Mexico as well, harken back, historically speaking, to the almost incredible Guadalupan events in Old Mexico. In fine, the story of the Lady of Guadalupe unwinds the skein of the dramatic history of the Spanish Empire in the fascinating New World that an intrepid Columbus gave graciously to Queen Isabella, in return for her trust and backing that she gave a dream-filled visionary.

The bold and daring conquest of Mexico is but the prelude to the dramatic history of New Mexico. Hernán Cortéz, defying orders of government officials, conquered the incredible Indian nations that he found in Mexico, in 1519. The rough-and-ready *conquistadores,* in whose veins ran the blood of stubborn Spaniards who had fought and out-witted and expelled the Moorish invaders in the Iberian peninsula, were not to be stopped by desperate Aztecs. Cortez had seen fabulous Indian kingdoms and he meant to make the most of the situation. As the soldier-chronicler Bernal Díaz del Castillo said so

2

aptly: "We came here to serve God and also to get rich."
All the new lands in the Americas were conquered and colonized "for both Majesties, God and King." So accompanying the adventurous *conquistadores* came the humble friar-sons of St. Francis. The first group of Franciscan *padres* were descriptively titled by the Indians as "the Twelve Apostles of Mexico," such was their zeal and humane treatment of the neophytes. *Motolinía,* which means "Poor Man," was what the Indians called the barefoot friars who, though poor in spirit, graciously shared the riches of hispanic culture wherever they evangelized for both God and King.

But despite the zealous challenge of Christianity and the patient ministry of the friars, while the *conquistadores,* in general, were human enough not to take advantage of the aborigines, there were rapacious hearts among them, and the endangering deeds of a few greedy Spaniards made the Christianization of the Indians almost impossible. But since the Americas would eventually blossom out into sovereign nations, it was unthinkable that Divine Province would not provide a way out of the anomalous situation that was arising between the Indians and the Spaniards.

It happened on Saturday, December 9th, 1531, only 12 years after Cortéz had finally conquered the Aztec Empire. Contemporary monuments and innumerable Indian and Spanish documents witness the historicity of the famous apparitions of the Virgin of Guadalupe. A Spanish priest, Tanco, basing his account upon the original history of the learned Aztec, Antonio Valeriano, a contemporary of the actual events, gives us this version:

"It was Saturday very early in the morning . . . and Juan Diego went in search of Christian learning, as revealed through divine doctrine." He was on his way to assist at the Saturday Mass in honor of the Virgin Mary, at Tlatelolco, one of the Franciscan missions.

"When he reached the top of the hillock called Tepeyac, dawn was breaking; and thence he heard strains of music coming. It sounded like the song of rare and wonderful birds. For an instant the singing ceased, and

3

then it seemed as if the mountains echoed with response.

"Startled, Juan Diego wondered whether he was dreaming, but a most pleasant voice broke his thoughtful reverie. 'Juanito, Juan Dieguito,' the voice called. Then he ventured to pursue the sound. He was not in the least frightened. On the contrary, he was filled with gladness, as he went up the hill to discover who was calling him. When he reached the summit, he saw a Lady of marvelous beauty, who was standing there serenely, and who motioned that he should approach.

"Once arrived within the radius of her presence, he greatly marveled at this, for there was something supernatural about it. Her garments were shining like the sun. The cliff on which she stood glittered with glory, like an anklet of precious stones, and illumined the earth like a rainbow. The mesquite, the prickly-pear, and other scrubby plants growing there took on an emerald hue. Their foliage changed to turquoise and their branches and thorns glistened like gold.

"He hearkened to her words . . . which were gentle and courteous, spoken after the manner of those addressed to one greatly esteemed. She said 'Juanito, the least of my sons, where art thou going?' He replied, 'My Lady and my Child, I must needs go to the church at Tlatelolco, to study the divine mysteries.' Immediately she resumed her discourse and revealed her wish.

" 'Know and take heed, thou, the least of my sons, that I am Holy Mary, Ever Virgin Mother of the True God for whom we live, the Creator of the World, Maker of Heaven and Earth. I urgently desire that a temple should be built to me here, to bear witness to my love, my compassion . . . my protection. For I am a merciful Mother to thee and to all thy fellow people on this earth who love me and trust me and invoke my help . . . Therefore, to realize all that my clemency claims, go to the Bishop of Mexico, and say that I sent thee to make manifest to him my great desire, namely, that here in the valley a temple should be built to me. Tell him word for

word all that thou hast seen and heard and admired. Be
assured that I shall be grateful and that I will reward
thee . . . Now thou has heard all my bidding, least of my
sons, go and do thy utmost.' "

The dramatic meeting of the Aztec Juan Diego and the
humble Bishop, Fray Juan de Zumárraga, — importer of the
printing press to the Americas, founder of the University of
Mexico, 'Defender of the Indians'—is fully documented in
both Indian and Spanish. The Bishop was startled to say the
least, and gently counselled the recent convert from paganism
to beware of illusions, and finally begged for a convincing sign
from the mysterious Lady at Tepeyac hill.

"Juan withdrew sad of heart because his statements went
unheeded, and the Lady's wishes seemed frustrated," Tanco's
account continues. But on his way home, the Lady was waiting
for Juan Diego at Tepeyac, and she soothed a sad heart. bidding him to return and again petition the bishop. A humbled
Juan Diego begged the Lady to send a Spaniard or some important Indian as messenger, but she insisted it should be he.

". . . On Tuesday, December 12th, Juan Diego rose
before dawn to fetch a priest for his dying uncle, Bernardino, who was suffering an account of malignant fever. . .
As he passed by Tepeyac, he remembered having forgotten to keep his appointment with the Lady the day previously, so he skirted the mountain, took a side path, and
hoped he wasn't seen.

"But there she was descending from the summit—
where he had first beheld her. She came to meet him on
the side of the hill . . . Without hesitation she gave her
instructions. 'Go, my son, to the summit of the hill . . .
where I give thee thy first orders. There you will find
some flowers. Gather them and assemble them. Then
fetch them hither.' " Juan Diego climbed Tepeyec hill and
"was astonished to find that quantities of exquisite Castillian roses were blooming there, and out of season, for
at this time of the year everything was frozen. They were
fragrant and covered with dewdrops." Gathering some
roses, Juan Diego put them into his *tilma* and headed

down to show the Lady. "She rearranged them in his cloak, and said: 'Least of my sons, this cluster of roses is the sign which you are to take to the Bishop. You are to tell him, in my name, that in them he will recognize my will and that he must fulfill it.' "

The climax was as dramatic as it was beautiful. When the Bishop welcomed Juan Diego, he asked to see the sign, noticing that Juan's *tilma* hid something from his servants. A miracle greater even than the Castillian roses was granted Juan Diego and the Bishop, for there on the woven yucca cloth was painted in striking colors the image of the Virgin of Guadalupe, exactly as she had appeared to Juan Diego four different times on Tepeyac hill.

The unique Guadalupan picture has been acclaimed by artists of world renown. The *tilma* of Juan Diego, on which the Image of the Virgin was impressed, was made of very coarse material and as loosely woven as sacking. This is one of the marvels of the Picture, for painters have declared, after a careful examination of it, that the material was not only not prepared, but was also unfit for preparation. They were baffled at the manner in which the colors were applied. No less mysterious do they find the apparent use of different mediums. Some parts appear to be done in oil, others in water color, still others in 'distemper,' while other tints are like those of flowers.

In 1851, the famous Mexican painter Miguel Cabrera, at the head of a commission of seven renowned artists, examined the Guadalupe Picture, and afterwards they declared jointly: "The plan of this Picture is so singular, so perfectly accomplished, and manifestly marvelous that whoever has any knowledge of the art of painting, on seeing it at once declares it a miraculous accomplishment . . . Its most beautiful grace of symmetry is a marvel that amazes those who are at all acquainted with sketching. Every line and turn of it is so clearly a marvel, that there actually shines forth in the admirable work the supreme power of its author."

The story of the Virgin of Guadalupe, and innumerable copies of the marvelous painting, came to New Mexico with the *conquistadores.* One of the earliest Franciscan missions, *El Paso del Norte* (now Juarez, Chihuahua) was given the patronal title of Our Lady of Guadalupe. The Indian *pueblo* church at Pojoaque, as also many humble northern New Mexican chapels still bear this name.

When Santa Fe's Patroness *la Conquistadora* came to New Mexico, in a caravan in 1625, the intrepid Padre Fray Alonzo de Benavides—one of the Southwest's great ecclesiastical leaders of colonial times—stopped with the caravanners —as was the custom—to say farewell to *La Guadalupana.*

Down through the centuries, cherishing and ever promoting devotion to Christ's Mother under the famous title of *La Virgen de Guadalupe,* Santa Fe continues to celebrate in *fiesta* fashion this Marian festival. The yearly novena of prayers and hymns, the vesper-services, never complete without the brightly burning *luminarias* and the flickering lights of countless *farolitos,* the large crowds of fervent devotees of Our Lady, the music of the organ and the joyous pealing of ancient bells, the noisy salutes of military fire, all this renews the spirit of Christianity which was enkindled by the marvelous apparitions of Our Lady to Juan Diego. And, linking millions of Christian hearts in public expression of hispanic culture and deep faith is the realization, that throughout the Americas, from Alaska to the tip of South America, the words of the late Pope Pius XII still hold true:

". . . On the *tilma* of poor Juan Diego was painted with brushes not of this world a most marvelous Picture, which the corrosive work of centuries was most wondrously to respect. The amiable Maiden asked for a See from which she might 'show and give all her love and compassion, help and protection . . . to all the inhabitants of that land and to all others who would invoke her and trust in her.' Since that historical moment the total evangelization has been accomplished. Furthermore, a banner was hoisted and a fortress has been erected against which the fury of all the storms would break. One of the fundamental pillars of the Faith in Mexico and in all the Americas was thus firmly established."

7

First Christmas Eve

St. Joseph looked about the beast-filled cave
And found some sticks and little bits of hay.
He built this meagre fuel into a flame
To warm the chilly corner where she lay.

She smiled at him with tired, lovely eyes
To thank him for his struggling little fire.
It warmed her heart far more than warmed the cave,
Just as her smile fulfilled his heart's desire.

Before their straw-filled mangers, drowsy oxen
Swayed slightly with a slow activity.
They rested on their feet, poor lowly things,
Not knowing night would bring Nativity.
—Mary Estelle Daunoy

CHAPTER 2

Las Posadas

Mary and Joseph Seek Shelter

Tradition is something vital that unites the past to the present and generates life for the future. The Spanish people are great believers in tradition, because it has well served them in the molding of their national and racial characteristics. Almost 2000 years ago, the Roman Empire engulfed the Iberian Peninsula as did also the teachings of Christ. And so Roman culture in its fullest sense, and the primitive simplicity of Christianity went hand in hand to mold the Spanish temperament. It is the great boast of the Spanish-speaking people even today to insist that their first instructor in the teachings of Jesus Christ was no other than the Apostle St. James the Greater, *Santiago,* whose patronage extends to all Spanish-speaking lands.

In the New World which the intrepid Cristóbal Colón graciously turned over to the greatest of Spanish monarchs, Isabela *la Catolica,* zealous Spanish missionaries were ever ready to pass on their European-Christian culture to the neophytes, the thousands upon thousands of Indians who were slowly but surely being civilized and christianized. But just as the Spaniards, through many centuries, had transformed Roman customs to suit their temperament, becoming as one historian so aptly described them as being "more Roman than Rome," so the Indians in the New World gave Christianity a new flavor based on their simple approach to life.

The 16th century had found Spain reaching heights in mysticism, in drama, in literature, in military prowess, in discovering and colonizing distant lands and peoples, feats of human endeavor that would be recorded as a Golden Age

9

in the history of the world. The 17th and 18th centuries would find New Spain (what we now know as Old Mexico), developing traditions of Christian worship that perdure today throughout many parts of the Spanish-speaking world. One of the most interesting contributions to Christianity is *Las Posadas,* that unique drama-representation of Mary and Joseph seeking shelter where they might prepare for Christ's birth.

For some reason or other too many English-speaking people tend to interpret many of our indo-hispanic traditions as something too exotic and foreign. Writer after writer extols the puzzling contradiction of the present day Indians in our many pueblos who on important patronal feastdays can mix very harmoniously what appears to be the strictly pagan with the devout Christian customs. Actually there is no contradiction whatsoever, unless one wants to deny the successful 'baptism' of many apparently Indian customs with European Christian traditions. The Catholic Church—who learned much from the Roman Empire, under which it suffered its birth pangs—has almost twenty centuries of experience in the forging of the truths of Christ's doctrines with the indigenous cultures that it has assimilated.

Las Posadas is a wonderful example of how an Indian love for dramatic representation served as a worthwhile vehicle for inculcating basic Christian truths; and, even though this custom was originated at first strictly for use among the varied Indian groups up and down Old Mexico, it was destined to spread throughout the entire Spanish-speaking world.

New Mexico is indeed fortunate in having preserved *Las Posadas* as part and parcel of its colorful Christmas customs. The tradition of representing Mary and Joseph in the seeking of shelter is a veritable contribution to the spirit of Christmas. As a sympathetic writer once interpreted the New Mexican yuletide customs: ". . . In no other region of the United States is Christmas so colorful and alive with contrast as it is in the Southwest. The treasures of this unique cultural heritage are on brilliant display during the season of the celebration of the birth of Christ, as at no other time of the year . . . they are like jewels of tradition which surround us like open sparkling treasure-chests, and all for us to savor and enjoy . . ."

The Spaniards—both the adventuresome *conquistadores* and the apostolic and fearless *padres*—loved drama and the public expression of Christian worship. And they knew how much it helped raise their minds and hearts to a more devout service of God. The medieval *Autos Sacramentales,* the mystery and miracle plays in the mother country, had been developed into great pieces of dramatic art. Now, a few generations later, the Spaniards realized that the Indians also loved pantomime and dramatic story-telling. So it is not hard to imagine an Augustinian friar in Old Mexico, who devised the rough script which was developed little by little into the present-day *Las Posadas.* This drama-representation of the search for lodging by Joseph and Mary is undoubtedly one of the most colorful and unique contributions of the New World to Old World Catholicism.

No one who has ever seen, or who has actively participated in the Mexican-style *Las Posadas* can forget the haunting simplicity of the Christmas gospel-story: Mary and Joseph seek lodging in Bethlehem, and human-nature being the same the world over, it re-enacts the presence of humaneness and niggardliness living side by side. Many people couldn't be bothered with two more weary pilgrims, but eventually someone was found who was big-hearted enough to provide, or suggest, some kind of rude shelter.

Las Posadas is based on the Christmas story-details as told and written by the evangelist St. Luke: "And it came to pass in those days that there went out a decree from Caesar Augustus that all the world should be enrolled. And all went to be enrolled, everyone into his own city . . . Joseph also went up from Galilee, out of the city of Nazareth, unto the city of David, which is called Bethlehem, because he was of the house and family of David, to be enrolled with Mary his espoused, who was with child. And it came to pass, that when they were there, her days were accomplished, that she should be delivered. And she brought forth her first-born Son, and wrapped Him up in swaddling clothes, and laid Him in a manger, BECAUSE THERE WAS NO ROOM FOR THEM

IN THE INN!" (Luke, 2, 1-14)

What better way to prepare the heart and mind for a soul-satisfying Christmas than to recreate the image of that anxious night when obedient, faithful Joseph feared he would not find a suitable place for Mary, "whose days were accomplished, that she should be delivered!"

The Mexican Indians loved variety—as did the Spaniards —and so even today there are many ways to act out *Las Posadas,* all depending, of course, on where and when it's held, and more importantly, depending on who is the director of the production. In general, this is the procedure followed almost everywhere. *Las Posadas* is presented in the form of a novena, which means that it will be re-enacted for nine consecutive nights before Christmas Eve, from December 16th through the 24th. Usually there are nine houses or neighborhood families who participate.

Gathering at a pre-determined place, at a church vestibule or at a particular home, the participants begin by singing the traditional Litany of the Blessed Virgin Mary, a series of praises to honor Mary the Mother of Christ; then follows the sung colloquy between the pilgrims (those on the 'outside') and the innkeeper and hosts (those on the 'inside'); usually a small boy will be chosen to carry a *santo* (a folk image in this case called by the Mexican people *un Misterio*) of St. Joseph, while a small girl carries the statue of Mary. The pilgrims knock and seek lodging, only to be refused, time after time, especially in the case where nine different homes are involved; then, moving from house to house, they continue their search, until at a pre-determined host-home, they are admitted with much rejoicing, while the *Misterios,* the folk-images of Mary and Joseph, are reverently placed on an especially arranged home-altar. And no people in the world are so ingenious as are the Mexican people in the elaborate preparations of artistic *nacimientos,* creche-scenes! Where the drama is acted out in the vestibule of a church, on being admitted inside, the images are placed on the altar or on a table placed in the sanctuary.

The music and the lyrics are simple, and are easily remembered. Where there are guests invited, the hosts provide for an extra copy so that all may follow the action with devotion. Usually everyone carries a lighted candle, and the flickering tapers add color and warmth to the seeking of lodging. After the solemn ceremonies, in some locales, a *piñata* party follows, and a fiesta is enjoyed by all, hosts and guests. And, typically Latin-style, some sort of eats and drinks are available for everybody, since traditional hospitality is part and parcel of *Las Posadas,* no matter how poor the host-family might be.

The following is a translation of the lyrics sung at *Las Posadas.* It is a very simple story, based on the details of the birth of Christ as written by St. Luke. A 'singing director' is usually in charge, and he takes his responsibility seriously, trying to harmonize all the different voices in a devoit presentation.

ENGLISH TRANSLATION OF LAS POSADAS

"The Pilgrims"
(The Entreaty)

From a very long journey,
We've arrived and are weary;
And come to implore you
For shelter this night.

Who will give us lodging,
To us, very weary travelers?
We are tired of walking,
And trudging so many roads.

We only intend to rob you
Of the kindness of your heart;
Permit my beloved spouse,
A corner in which to rest!

But our's is a grave necessity,
To beg at least some shelter,
For my wife needs a room,
In which to seek repose!

But, oh, do take heed,
For the love of God Himself!
My beloved spouse is cold,
And getting more fatigued!

But this beautiful Maiden,
No longer can withstand the cold;
She will not be able to withstand,
Weather which becomes more inclement!

The night quickly advances,
In God's name be compassionate!
Do provide some simple rest,
For the Queen of Heaven!

But, 'tis only Joseph, and Mary,
His most beloved spouse,
Who, here standing at your door,
Have come seeking lodging!

Slight is not the hospitality you offer
For this kindness, God Himself,
Will certainly recompense you,
From heaven will reward you well!

Let happiness and much joy abide,
In this our humble abode, today!
For the travellers are none other,
Than a loving spouse named Joseph,
With a chaste and lovely Maiden!

"The Innkeeper"
(The Response)

Who comes to our door,
On such a cold night?
Who approaches impudently,
And disturbs our rest?

Who is it that makes such requests?
I cannot heed such a demand,
For you might just be thieves,
And bent on robbing me!

Actually there is no room,
In the inn that is empty;
But the countryside is free,
And there's hospitality there!

Who is it that disturbs our rest?
And bothers us now in the night?
Go away, go away, please,
And stop robbing us of sleep!

Oh, you stubborn people,
You are getting most annoying!
Please depart from this place,
And stop robbing us of sleep!

Certainly you know how late it is!
And coming with such a request,
Makes us all the more suspicious!
Go away at once!

Your entreaties do annoy us,
And we shall no longer listen;
Seek but an empty field,
And find some shelter there!

Then enter, most beautiful Maiden!
Thou and thy Spouse, please come in!
For this is thy house, believe me,
And most humbly do we offer it thee!

Open wide these doors and portals,
Do away with all suspicions,
For here has come to seek repose,
The blessed Queen of Heaven!

And since we've been so highly honored,
Assuredly we must perforce give thanks,
Humble thanks we do now give,
To Joseph and to Mary.

13

Little Fires

The little fires that blaze on Christmas Eve
Are lit by simple folks whose hearts believe
The Christ Child wanders softly through the night
And blesses all who set a guiding light.
    (O Little Child, I tend my fire and pray
      For fires around the world to guide Thy way.)
                    —Dorothy Linney

(Reprinted courtesy New Mexico Magazine)

CHAPTER 3

Farolitos Are Not Luminarias!

No other Christmas custom has so vividly captured the imagination of countless visitors to Santa Fe than the traditional lighting which is commonly called *farolitos*. Perhaps this form of holiday lighting catches the eye so forcibly, because one sees them everywhere, on church walls and roof, on humble adobe dwellings, in beautiful formations on sidewalks and outlining the homes of the wealthy, on roofs and walls of public buildings; everywhere these mellow lights illumine the scene and invite all who see them to get into the Christmas spirit. The glow from the flickering candles inside the brown paper-sacks sets a mood of peace and quiet, and inspires reverence and simplicity. There is nothing elaborate or fancy or expensive about these *farolitos,* and yet they serve the purpose; they aptly promote and enhance the mood and spirit of the coming of the Messiah, the birth of the Christ Child.

Not only do the thousands upon thousands of glowing *farolitos* on Christmas Eve remind the northern New Mexican people of a tradition with sacred meaning rooted in a cultural past that has much to offer to the future, but despite our apparent indifference to a more active promotion of such unique, picturesque customs, the lighting up of these quaint little 'lanterns' has spread to many parts of the United States. One such surprising instance was in a small community in Oklahoma, where a matron utilizes the idea of *farolitos* not only at Christmas, but for any and all kinds of social gatherings at night. This lady, when asked where she had learned of this form of lighting, reminisced of several happy visits at the Otero's *Placita Chamisos* in Santa Fe.

And since this colorful custom of Christmas lighting is here to stay, since the Spanish-speaking people up and down the *Rio Grande del Norte* have come to appreciate the inherent value of passing on to future generations the spiritual and cultural beauty of an ancient heritage, and since the Anglo is to be thanked for promoting a beautiful custom as valuable Americana, it behooves me to interpret the background of the *farolitos* as distinct from that other more ancient and venerable custom called the *luminaria*. The distinction between these two unique holiday forms of lighting is made, simply and honestly, not for the vain attempt at being pedantic, but to enhance the beauty of both the *farolitos* and the *luminarias* by setting their origin in their proper historical and cultural perspectives.

Several years ago, when the Old Santa Fe Association decided to emphasize the traditional lighting of the Christmas *farolitos* and *luminarias,* I was happily editing the venerable Spanish weekly EL NUEVO MEXICANO, the last stronghold of many a fast-disappearing treasury of folklore. Under the leadership of Ina Sizer Cassidy, the OSFA was determined to give authentic interpretation to the origin of both the *farolitos* and the *luminarias*. Seeing such wholehearted enthusiasm for customs that should have ordinarily meant much to our hispanic ancestral culture, I started to dig up bits of information that eventually led me to serious research in early Spanish colonial history. Little by little, I began to fit together the pieces of the mosaic that told the unique story of both of these customs.

Now, for the sake of contributing a little grain of sand to the foundation that formed the basis of that colorful and dramatic history which is our legacy, I offer, in all simplicity of heart, the information available on the *farolito* and the *luminaria*. Perhaps the reasoning behind my contribution is the wisdom that permeates the classic definition of humility which characterized the life and influence of one of the greatest of all Spaniards, the mystic and reformer, Santa Teresa de Jesús de Avila. Her whole philosophy of life is epitomized in this: "Humility is nothing else but a continuous walking toward Truth."

The Luminaria Came First

Tracing the history of the *luminaria* I came across many instances where historians and folklorists generally agree that the *luminarias,* the 'little fires,' date back to the first *Noche Buena* in faraway Belén, to the down-to-earth practical fires that the shepherds needed to keep themselves warm and the light necessary to keep away wolves and thieves that might endanger their flocks of sheep. Undoubtedly, these *hogueras,* or bonfires, were brightly lit when the Angel of the Lord suddenly disconcerted the simple shepherds with his celestial message: "Fear not, for behold I bring you good tidings of great joy, that shall be to all the people; for this day is born to you a Saviour, Who is Christ the Lord, in the City of David . . ."

Another primary source of history in Mexican archives further elucidates the story of the shepherds' fires and goes back into the ancient Roman history of Spain. In pre-Christian times the pagan peoples of what is today Spain, prepared huge bonfires and lit them on hills and mountain-tops to celebrate the feasts dedicated to ancient gods and goddesses. And when Christianity was brought into Spain by none other than one of Christ's twelve apostles, St. James the Greater, and known to all Spanish-speaking peoples as *Santiago,* it was inevitable that the Christianized Spaniards 'baptize' the ancient pagan fires to serve the cause of Christianity. The shepherds' fires on the first *Noche Buena* were enough of an excuse to 'convert' pagan customs into practical Christian usage.

Fascinating research in the early colonial history of Old Mexico, that fabulous country designated by adventurous Spaniards as *La Nueva España,* continues the interesting story of the *luminaria* in the New World. As indomitable colonizers of a far-flung world empire, the *conquistadores* and the zealous *padres* needed no outside prodding to introduce customs that formed part and parcel of everyday living in the mother country. Permit me to share some delightful bits of 16th century history in colonial Mexico, so that the origin of the traditional *luminarias* in the New World will add even more lustre to your Christmas lighting in the future.

In the first group of Franciscan *padres* that came into Old Mexico in 1524, that apostolic band of missionaries which was descriptively entitled by the Mexican Indians 'The Twelve Apostles of Mexico,' one of their number was eventually commanded by the ecclesiastical authorities to write down an exact account of the missionary endeavors before they became lost to posterity. Padre Fray Toribio de Motolinía was not a man to let grass grow under his feet. He set to work immediately, in 1536, and put into writing, as best he could, what had occurred since the Franciscan *padres'* coming in 1524, and with great detail recounted current events of importance and interest.

Motolinía's book, which is entitled HISTORY OF THE INDIANS OF NEW SPAIN, is an indispensable source of information on the history of the Franciscan missions in New Spain. It is as valuable a source of Church History in the New World as is his contemporary Franciscan-brother, Padre Fray Bernardino de Sahagún's HISTORY OF ANCIENT MEXICO with reference to the best interpretation ever written on Aztec culture.

Motolinía writes:

". . . The Indians celebrate the feast of the Lord, of Our Lady and of the principal Patron Saints of the towns with much rejoicing and solemnity. They decorate their churches very tastefully with what ornaments they are able to get, and their lack of tapestry they make up for with tree branches, flowers, reed mace and sedge. These they spread on the ground, together with leaves of mint which has thriven incredibly in this land.

"Where a procession is to pass they erect numerous triumphal arches made of roses and adorned with trimmings and garlands of the same flowers. The wreaths of flowers they fashion are very attractive. This is the reason why in this land everybody is bent on having rose gardens. It has happened that, if they have no roses, they send ten or twelve leagues for them to the towns of the warm climate where roses are nearly always in bloom and have a very sweet odor.

"Attired in white shirts and mantles and bedecked in feathers and with a bouquet of roses in their hands, the Indian lords and chiefs perform a dance and sing in their language the songs that solemnize the feast which they are celebrating. The friars have translated these songs for them . . . and the Indian masters have put them into the meter to which the Indians are accustomed. The songs are graceful and harmonious. In many places the dancing and singing begin at midnight, and numerous *luminarias* illumine the *patios*. The *patios* in this land are very spacious and are excellently kept because, the number of people being large and the churches too small to accomodate them, the chapels, *capillas abiertas*, are outside in the *patio*, arranged in such a way that all the Indians may attend the Holy Mass . . ."

La Noche Buena

"On Christmas night the Indians place many *luminarias* in the *patios* of the churches and on the terraces of their houses. Since there are many flat-roofed houses, and these extend a league or two, the scene resembles the starry skies. Generally the Indians sing, beat drums and ring bells . . . On Christmas night the Indians come to the divine services and attend three Masses . . . They also carry torches (*achones*, perhaps, like they still do at Taos!), which are made of pitch-pine, are firmly tied together, and these torches produce a good light . . . they hold the torches in order to furnish light . . ."

Motolinía's HISTORY OF THE INDIANS OF NEW SPAIN is indeed a treasure-house of information, not only of the customs observed by the Indians with regard to 'Christian Holydays of Obligations—Festive Decorations for Christmas . . .' etc., but, more importantly, many of the missionary teaching methods that were later to be used in the faraway 'ancient Kingdom of the New Mexico' and in Arizona, in Florida, Virginia, Georgia, and later on in Baja and Alta

Californias; wherefore the more successful missionary methods had their origin in the experimentation done in Motolinía's time.

To truly appreciate much of the beauty of the Spanish and Indian festivals and customs in New Mexico, we have no alternative but to search for their origin in history books similar in scope to Motolinía's, otherwise we are depriving future generations of a cultural heritage which is unique and fascinating.

The Farolitos Came Later!

Many are the sincere writers and journalists in New Mexico who do their best to promote the usage of the colorful *farolitos* and the fast-disappearing *luminarias*. But unfortunately, either through sheer ignorance(used here not to mean stupidity, but rather 'lack of due knowledge' historical or cultural!), or sometimes through the more easy way of copying other people's mistakes, the distinction is not made, and many people who would like to know more about the origin of the *luminarias* and the *farolitos* seem to get more confused as the years go by. Even folklorists sometimes forget the inherent value of doing serious research, and little by little the true story is lost irretrievably. But there's a rather simple solution in the promoting of traditions which should mean something for New Mexico: this interpretation is based strictly on primary historical sources through assiduous research in archives and books of worth, plus the living 'folk mouth' as it has been transmitted from generation to generation.

The *farolitos* have a story all their own to tell! Studying the history of the Spanish Empire as a whole, the patterns of administrations, commerce, architecture, religious customs, art, missionary movements, all of these interweave to form a unique system of discovery and colonization. That is why when prospective *conquistadores* left the mother-land for a place in *Las Indias* (The Indies, or otherwise known as The

New World), they could come to Mexico, Guatemala, Chile, Argentina, Columbia, Peru, anywhere in the empire, and feel right at home. In much the same way, today, any Spanish-speaking native of New Mexico can travel south of the border and find a cultural atmosphere that reminds him of home. Thus it was in this cultural atmosphere that the origin of the *farolito* has a meaning that is worthwhile.

It was in *Las Islas Filipinas* (the Philippine Islands) that the *farolito* took on a flavor that was to be passed down to us New Mexicans. Briefly, the story is something like this. There was considerable commercial activity between the Spanish Philippines and China, and this commerce was naturally profitable to both countries, so much so that soon a cultural atmosphere was developed which served to promote the sharing of ideas. The Chinese had for centuries made festive lighting a thing of great beauty, the Spanish-traders liked what they saw, and inevitably use of the Chinese custom of colorful lanterns became a reality in the Islands. From the Philippines the idea came to Mexico, the same as did the priceless ivory *Cristos,* statuary and cloth and spices, through the port of Acapulco and on into the interior.

In Mexico today, for practically any type of *fiesta,* especially the church festivals and the gala occasions of the humble people, imitations of Chinese lanterns are profusely utilized both in and out of churches and in *patios* and homes. The Mexican artisans have developed the making of festive lanterns into a great art, and the temperate climate serves to promote such elaborate and delicate lighting.

Eventually, the idea of festive *farolitos* — in the sense of lanterns, and not as bonfires! — came up north from Mexico. Just as *La Conquistadora,* the most precious heirloom of New Mexico's Spanish Colonial epoch, came up to Santa Fe in an ox-cart, so the *farolitos* found a new home. But such fragile lanterns were so few and far between, that the *Neomejicanos* soon learned a lesson, that these expensive *farolitos de papel de China,* the delicate lanterns made of Chinese paper or fragile materials, just would not last too long here. But the idea had taken hold of people's imaginations. The Chinese lanterns that came on the tri-annual wagon caravans from Old Mexico would not last more than one season, perhaps, but with a little ingenuity, other more hardy materials could be used instead!

And so it was, when paper bags became available when the *Americanos* came over the Santa Fe Trail and brought all kinds of merchandise to sell in the old town's dusty *plaza,* the Spanish women had found what they needed, sturdy brown bags which could be improvised into lanterns for happy *fiesta* parties. (In much the same way did the famous tinwork originate from sheer necessity; crude materials were becoming available, and crude materials were much better than nothing at all.) Only the courageous tenacity of the Spanish people kept the festive *farolito* from disappearing. And the effective lighting that it is today, the simplicity and ingenuity of construction, the availability of inexpensive materials, all of this serves its purpose. Christmas-time, with its emphasis on the primitive simplicity of the manger-cave-stable serves as a veritable challenge for festive lighting that enhances the great *fiesta de la Navidad del Niño Jesus.*

Conclusions About Farolitos and Luminarias!

Luminarias have a purpose all their own. Just as the shepherds lit their bonfires to keep warm and to safeguard the safety of their flocks, the 'baptism' of these shepherds' fires evokes memories of hispanic culture which are sacred. The liturgy of the Catholic Church, time after time, calls Christ the 'Light of the World,' and on seeing these *hogueras,* the warmth-giving bonfires, the mind and the heart and the soul are elevated to meditation on the most important event in the history of the world, the fruitful coming of the Messiah.

The *farolitos* are a festive lighting, a heart-warming illumination that reiterates that joyous message of the angels: "Glory to God in the highest, and on earth peace to men of good will." The *farolitos* are an invitation to join in the holiday spirit of peace of mind and heart, a beckoning to participate ever more fully in the festive atmosphere of Christ's birthday. As a Christmas form of illumination it enhances the primitive simplicity of the *luminarias,* whose centuries-long usefulness is still a necessity in the rural countryside of New Mexico. No one can visit such places as Truchas, Cordova, Trampas and Chimayó, and not sense the timeliness of the *luminaria,* not only as festive lighting but as the spiritual need for belongingness. Someday, perhaps, the *luminaria* will no longer seem to be needed, but by then its use will have become an integral part of truly American folk-artistry.

ROMANCE IX

Del Nacimiento

The Birth of Christ

Ya que era llegado el tiempo
En que de nacer había,
Así como desposado
De su tálamo salía

Abrazado con su esposa,
Que en sus brazos la traía,
Al cual la graciosa Madre
En un pesebre ponía,

Entre unos animales
Que a la sazón allí había;
Los hombres decían cantares,
Los ángeles melodía,

Festejando el desposorio
Que entre tales dos había;
Pero Dios en el pesebre
Allí lloraba y gemía,

Que eran joyas que la esposa
Al desposorio traía;
Y la Madre estaba en pasmo
De que tal trueque veía;

El llanto del hombre en Dios,
Y en el hombre la alegría,
Lo cual del uno y del otro
Tan ajeno ser solía.

—San Juan de la Cruz
(1542-1591)

Now that the season was approaching
Of His long-expected birth,
Like a bridegroom from his chamber
He emerged upon our earth

Clinging close to His beloved
Whom He brought along with Him.
While the gracious Mary placed them
In a manger damp and dim.

Amongst the animals that round it
At that season stretched their limbs,
Men were singing songs of gladness
And the angels chanting hymns,

To celebrate the wondrous marriage
By whose bond such two were tied,
But the wee God in the manger
He alone made moan and cried;

Tears were the jewels of the dowry
Which the bride with her had brought.
And the Mother gazed upon them
Nearly fainting at the thought.

The tears of Man in God alone,
The joy of God in men was seen.
Two things as alien to each other,
Or to the rule, had never been.

—Saint John of the Cross
(1542-1591)

La Noche Buena

This Is Christmas Eve!

". . . But three days later came the great feast of Christmas, and the birth of life and purity in the world. All worked hard, and rededicated themselves in the midst of hazard, loneliness and loss; and resolve grew with the preparation for war . . . On a cold December night sentries reported hostile announcements . . . The Governor, Don Juan de Oñate, personally took charge of doubling sentinels on guard . . . *Luminarias* were lighted to see by and to keep warm, for it was indeed a very cold night . . . . . . But Christmas came and with it a new wagontrain from Mexico. It arrived at the capital — at San Juan de los Caballeros — on Christmas Eve, bringing new families, new soldiers, six new friars, quantities of arms and ammunition, blankets and clothing, and shoes for everyone. Bonfires of celebration were lighted, and there was music and singing, and at midnight everyone went to Mass (*la Misa del Gallo*) to give humble thanksgiving . . ." —Paul Horgan, THE GREAT RIVER

Long ago, in 1598, when the Spaniards colonized the northern part of New Mexico, it was inevitable that the first Christmas spent on the new frontier was going to be one that they would never forget. Settled, temporarily, only a few hundred yards from an Indian *pueblo,* there is no doubt that the Spaniards experienced mixed feelings. In the last resort, perhaps only hispanic pride and the comforts of religion, interwoven with sheer courage and a healthy fear of the future, united them inextricably in the spirit of a Christmas 'rededication.'

But it was *la Noche Buena,* and although Christmas is primarily a time for rejoicing over the coming of the infant Redeemer, there is a note of sadness running through this symphony of joy. The physical discomfort of the Nativity cave, the fact that only the poor of the earth bothered to attend His birth, these hard little nuggets of reality seem to foreshadow the final destiny of the Christ Child. "The real Son of God by nature became Man that men might become sons of God by adoption." The Christian background of these lonely, pioneering Europeans came to the fore. It was the 'Good Night' — Christmas Eve — and bonfires of celebration were lighted, and there was music and singing, and at midnight everyone went to *la Misa del Gallo!*

People who know enough Spanish to be able to translate *la Misa del Gallo* into 'the Mass of the Rooster' sometimes wonder just what connection a rooster has to do with the Christmas Midnight Mass. Since *los animalitos de Dios* — as San Isidro, the Farmer, used to call all the animals of creation — undoubtedly have a reason to praise God by their very existence and their harmonious relation with nature itself, the Spanish people never thought it strange to associate the rooster with Christmas.

The Latin-American people, in general, enjoy fixing up elaborate creche-scenes for the Christmas season, and barnyard fowl have just as much a right to be represented at the manger as the camel. At any rate, one of the choice bits of folklore surrounding the birth of Christ is the presence of the alert rooster.

As my grandmother used to tell us, when my brothers and I were small children, it seems that on the night that Jesus was born, since there weren't any visitors to the crib, the *animalitos* took it upon themselves to make up for the lack of human kindness. Inside the cave, quietly doing their part, were the ox and the donkey, both providing warmth for the Christ Child with their breath. And outside the nativity-cave-stable, a rooster flew up to the highest point he could find near the manger, and raising his crown proudly up in the cold night air, he began to announce the good tidings of Christ's birth. This rooster in his best voice sang out loud and clear *Cristo nació!* which means: 'Christ has been born!' And, the folklorish story continues, another rooster answered the cry with his contribution. The second rooster crowed happily: *En Belén!* which translates into the prophetic answer truly Messianic in scope: 'In Bethlehem!' And so, putting the happy crowing of two roosters together, the Spanish speaking people believe that 'for Almighty God nothing is impossible' and especially at the birth of God's Divine Son. Thus the legend of the rooster (Christ has been born! In Bethlehem!) became a handy tale to hinge onto the liturgical name of one of the three solemnized masses celebrated at Christmas: the Midnight Mass, the Mass of Dawn (undoubtedly the origin of letting a crowing rooster announce the beginning of a new day), and the Third Mass, late on Christmas day.

But despite the fact that the name *Misa del Gallo* might possibly be a misnomer, it does not disturb us Spanish-speaking people, for we do not mind sharing an interesting folklore tale with Almighty God; for is not Christmas, the birthday of Jesus Christ, and the coming of the Messiah into the world, the most important event the world has ever known?

But all the penitential spirit of the season called Advent, the spiritual preparation for Christ's birth, the traditional decorations and quaint customs, the carol-singing, and the buying and giving of gifts, the lighting of *farolitos* and *luminarias,* the preparation of special foods and delicacies, even the presence of Santa Claus as an intermediary in the gift-giving, everything which comprises what we know to mean 'getting into the Christmas spirit,' to the devout Spanish-speaking people, all of this is but the means to the end: to be ready in heart and soul for the choice blessings and graces to be received at the liturgical celebration of Christ's birth — the Christmas Mass. Everything that went before would be in vain if the heart and mind and soul were not receptive to the graces of the *Misa de Navidad.*

Since the liturgy of the Catholic Church is 'the working out of the virtue of religion on the social level,' it necessarily

27

follows that to Catholics 'the liturgy is the official prayer and worship that the Church offers to God, and it centers around the Mass and the sacraments.' All things being equal, praying and worshiping through the liturgy is much more efficacious than private prayer because Christ is present at every liturgical function. In his famous encyclical *Mediator Dei,* the late Pope Pius XII wrote: "Christ is present at the august Sacrifice of the altar both in the person of His minister and above all under the Eucharistic species. He is present in the Sacraments, infusing into them the power which makes them ready instruments of sanctification."

Thus, it is not hard to understand how all the traditional customs that surround the celebration of Christmas among the Spanish-speaking have as their object to elevate and prepare the heart and mind and soul of the Christian for an effective participation in the Christmas Mass. *La Misa del Gallo* is the climax of the joyful Christmas celebration, and Christmas Eve, *la Noche Buena,* is the proximate preparation for a worthy reception of the Sacraments of Penance and the Holy Eucharist. Attendance at one of the Christmas masses — since every priest has the unique privilege of celebrating three masses on Christmas! — is the highlight of *la Navidad,* and then it is that the Spanish-speaking enjoy singing that famous traditional *villancico* (Christmas carol) which is ever so old and yet always so new:

"Vamos todos a Belén Con amor y gozo, Adoremos al Señor Nuestro Redentor"	"Let's all go to Bethlehem With love and great joy, Let us all adore Our Lord, Who is our Redeemer"

The Midnight Mass

INTROIT. Ps. 2.7 The Lord hath said to Me: Thou art My Son, this day have I begotten Thee. Ps. 2,1. Why have the Gentiles raged, and the people devised vain things? V. Gloria . . .

COLLECT: O God, Who has brightened this most holy night with the shining of the true light, grant, we beseech Thee, that we may enjoy in heaven the delights of Him whose mystical light we have known on earth. Who with

Thee liveth and reigneth in the unity of the same Holy Ghost, God, world without end. Amen.

EPISTLE. Titus 2,11-15: Lesson from the Epistle of blessed Paul the Apostle to Titus.

Dearly beloved, the grace of God our Saviour hath appeared to all men, instructing us, that, denying ungodliness and worldly desires, we should live soberly, and justly, and godly in this world, looking for the blessed hope and coming of the glory of the great God and our Saviour Jesus Christ, Who gave Himself for us, that He might redeem us from all iniquity, and might cleanse to Himself a people acceptable, a pursuer of good works. These things speak, and exhort: In Christ Jesus our Lord.

GRADUAL. Ps. 109, 3,1: With Thee is the principality in the day of Thy strength in the brightness of the saints, from the womb before the day-star I begot Thee. V. The Lord said to my Lord: Sit Thou at My right hand, until I make Thy enemies Thy footstool. Alleluia, alleluia. V. Ps. 2, 7. The Lord hath said to Me: Thou are My Son, this day have I begotten Thee. Alleluia.

GOSPEL, Luke 2, 1-14: Continuation of the holy Gospel according to St. Luke. At that time, there went out a decree from Caesar Augustus, that the whole world should be enrolled. This enrolling was first made by Cyrinus, the governor of Syria. And all went to be enrolled, every one into his own city. And Joseph also went up from Galilee out of the city of Nazareth, into Judea to the city of David, which is called Bethlehem, because he was of the house and family of David, to be enrolled with Mary his espoused wife, who was with child. And it came to pass that when they were there, her days were accomplished, that she should be delivered. And she brought forth her firstborn Son, and wrapped Him up in swaddling clothes, and laid Him in a manger, because there was no room for them in the inn. And there were in the same country shepherds watching, and keeping the night watches over their flock. And behold an angel of the Lord stood by them, and the brightness of God shone round about them, and they feared with a great fear. And the angel said to them: Fear not; for behold I bring you good tidings of great joy, that shall be to all the people; for this day is born to you a Saviour, Who is Christ the Lord, in the city of David. And this shall be a sign unto you: You shall find the infant wrapped in swaddling clothes, and laid in a manger. And suddenly there was with the angel a multitude of the heavenly army, praising God, and saying: Glory to God in the highest; and on earth peace to men of good will.

OFFERTORY. Ps. 95, 11-13: Let the heavens rejoice, and let the earth be glad before the face of the Lord, because He cometh.

SECRET: May the oblation of this day's festivity, we pray Thee, O Lord, find acceptance with Thee; that, by the bounty of Thy grace, we may, through this sacred intercourse, be found made like unto Him in Whom our substance is united with Thee. Who with Thee . . .

COMMUNION. Ps. 109, 3: In the brightness of the saints, from the womb before the day-star I begot Thee.

POSTCOMMUNION: Grant, we beseech Thee, O Lord our God, that we, who rejoice to celebrate with these mysteries the nativity of our Lord Jesus Christ, may deserve by worthy living to attain His companionship. Who with Thee . . .

Today A Shepherd

Today a shepherd and our kin,
O Gil, to random us is sent,
And He is God Omnipotent.

For us hath He cast down the pride
And prison wall of Satanás;
But He is of the kin of Bras,
Of Menga, also of Llorent.
Oh, is not God Omnipotent?

If He is God, how then is He
Come hither and here crucified?
—With His dying sin also died,
Enduring death the innocent.
Gil, how omnipotent God is!

Why, I have seen Him born, pardie
And of a most sweet shepherdess.
—If He is God, how can He be
With such poor folk as these content?
—Seest not He is Omnipotent?

Give over idle parleyings
And let us serve Him, you and I,
And since He came on earth to die,
Let us die with Him too, Llorent;
For He is God Omnipotent!

—Santa Teresa de Avila
(1515-1582)

Typically Spanish in feeling, Santa Teresa uses a pastoral theme for this Christmas poem. Gil, Bras, Menga, Llorent are names of shepherds, colorful imaginary names that suited poetic license.

CHAPTER 5

Los Pastores

Unique Medieval Mystery Drama

Assuredly as Christmasy as mistletoe, or the favorite evergreen tree all decorated gaily with colored lights and beautiful ornaments; and certainly more typically New Mexican in spirit, is the story of the fascinating medieval miracle plays which still abound in different parts of the state. To enrich this year's Christmas spirit, perhaps a commentary on the history of *Los Pastores,* the most popular of mystery Christmas plays, will be appropriate, especially since a 'renaissance' of this unique drama has been initiated in the Española Valley, much to the delight of both young and old.

To enjoy *El Coloquio de Los Pastores* in the romantic mission atmosphere of the ancient church of the rustic village of Trampas, in the shadows of the towering Truchas Peak, on a cold winter's night, with blazing *luminarias* in the courtyard, while inside the pot-bellied stoves are surrounded by the expectant villagers, and the haunting melodies of the songs of the 'shepherds,' is an experience worth a lifetime!

In her centuries-old religious folk plays, New Mexico has preserved for posterity a literary heritage which is a significant part of our American civilization and culture. The early mystery plays, composed in flamboyant verse in archaic Spanish, have been passed down by word of mouth from generation to generation. And the impact of the evolution of the language is ever so obvious, so typically folklorish, the popular style of the common-language of the peasant-folk has made its subconscious entry into the medieval script of the mystery play.

There are no printed originals, for they live 'in the folk

mouth.' Collectors have transcribed these plays as they were recited to them, after diplomatic coaxing, by the native impresarios, or they have obtained them by studying the old hand-worn *cuadernos* (notebooks) sometimes made by some interested outsider in the last few generations. These handwritten copies in the well-thumbed notebooks are guarded as sacredly as family heirlooms.

There is indeed a unique spirit in New Mexico — the Land of Enchantment, no less! — which certainly lends itself to the perservation of the old traditional customs and ancient folklore. Perhaps no one who has ever written of New Mexico has expressed in words more of the true spirit of this dramatic land than Charles Fletcher Lummis, friend and interpreter of the Southwest: for he wrote, "Sun, silence, and adobe — that is New Mexico in three words. If a fourth word were needed, it need be only to clinch the three. It is the great American Mystery — the United States which is not the United States."

Undoubtedly, part of that "American Mystery" is the preservation of this religious drama of the people through centuries of conquest and hard struggle, the joys and sorrows of a people in a land that was yet to be reconquered definitely! This rich deposit of hispanic folk drama is found also in parts of Florida, Texas, Colorado, Arizona and in California, but it is in 'the Ancient Kingdom of the New Mexico' that it seems to have taken its deepest root. A piece of literature, whether it be a ballad, a lyric poem or epic, a romance, a tale or drama, survives only because it appeals to the innermost feelings of the people, and it is preserved and treasured because it is definitely a link with the past that is not soon to be forgotten.

Fray Pedro de Gante, who established the 16th century *Colegio de San Francisco* in Mexico City, wrote back to the Emperor-King of Spain, Charles V, telling him of the successful attempts of the missionaries to introduce the old Spanish customs among the native-tribes: "When the great feast of Christmas was approaching, I had invited all the Indians for twenty leagues around, to come to the celebration of the Nativity of Christ our Redeemer . . . The place was so crowded that there was not enough room for all who came, in the church *patio*."

The methods instituted by Fray Pedro de Gante in his school were soon imitated in nearly all the Indian schools established by the zealous missionaries. The *Padres*, noting the great pleasure the Indians experienced in participating in their many and varied ceremonial dances, grafted the Christian ideal of festive celebration on to the existing native penchant for elaborate ceremonial. Many missionaries noticed the colorful pantomimic dances and were inspired to utilize the descriptive native customs for purposes of instruction in the Christian Faith.

Thus, the Indian love of drama was put to better use — the celebration of Christian feasts as a substitute for the pagan ceremonies, which did not abet the teachings of Christian morality. The missionaries, therefore, did not forbid all the Indian customs, but they did try to convert or 'baptize' them to the Christian culture. From such a source as this, undoubtedly, was developed the beautiful religious dance-drama which is still performed today in New Mexican villages and pueblos, *Los Matachines*.

Simultaneously with the drama of evangelization, most of which was written and performed in the native languages, there were produced the *Autos Sacramentales* — medieval mystery plays — which were such an integral part of the Spanish celebration of the Feast of Corpus Christi intermittently from the 13th to the 18th centuries.

Some of the religious plays produced in Old Mexico in the 16th century were brought directly from the Mother-Country (Spain) by the missionaries and the *conquistadores*, and used in their original form. Others were translated by the *padres* themselves into the native languages, or adapted by them from the already existing Spanish drama to suit their particular purpose.

Fray Toribio de Motolinía wrote in descriptive detail the customs and manner of celebration and decoration for Christmas and many other Indian festivals. His book THE HISTORY OF THE INDIANS IN NEW SPAIN contains many references, too numerous to quote here, concerning the missionary activities: the teaching of instrumental music, singing, the drama, and the colorful details of indo-hispanic pageantry. Fray Toribio's descriptions of the Christmas celebrations, in particular, leave little doubt in the mind of the student of the religious drama and folklore that, the traditional celebrations still existent in New Mexico today have their origin and counterpart in 16th century *Nueva España* (Old Mexico, as it was then called). Padre Motolinía wrote of Christmas Eve:

"The night of the Nativity of Our Lord (Christmas Eve), they (the Indians) are accustomed to place many *luminarias* (bonfires) in the *patios* of the churches, and even on some of the flat roofs of the houses, so that since their houses join one to the other, the bonfires light the whole street, sometimes even as much as a league, the whole impression is that of a brightly lit sky . . .

"They all go to Midnight Mass . . . where there is a *Nacimiento* (creche) which remains in the church until after Kings' Day. This represents Bethlehem with the Child Jesus, His Mother Mary and St. Joseph . . . They celebrate also with great festivity the Kings' Day, *el Día de Los Reyes Magos,* and represent the drama of the gift offerings to the Christ Child. And on other days they commemorate similar passages from the story of our redemption."

Yet another friar-missionary, Fray Alonso Ponce, gives us more explicit details as regards the Christmas season. This *padre* was a Commissary of the Franciscan missions of New Spain and Visitor of the Province of his Order. In his chronicles of the events which occurred during a thorough visitation of the missions under his immediate care, he describes a play presented by the Indians of Tlaxamuclo, and the year was 1578. From this account it is easy to recognize the lineage of *Los Pastores* and also the play called *Los Reyes Magos.*

"In the *patio* of the church, high up near the belfry, was the *portal de Belén* (the manger scene) in which was

placed the Christ Child, His Mother Mary and St. Joseph.
. . . Somewhere apart from the *nacimiento* was an arbor
in which King Herod was seated in an arm chair . . .
From a hill behind the town descended the Three Kings
on horseback . . . With them was an Indian on foot, and
behind them came an old Indian of 80 years (chosen
for this part because of his venerable age), bearing the
gifts which were to be offered to the Christ Child . . .
While the Kings were descending the hill, some children
dressed as angels danced and sang *coplas* in the Mexican
language . . . Then came a dance of the shepherds, each
bearing their gourds and shepherd' pouches, their crooks,
and other pastoral trappings, even though they were
very poor . . .

"An angel appeared intoning 'Gloria in Excelsis
Deo,' and giving the news of the birth of the Christ Child
. . . The shepherds dazed by all this, but coming to themselves, hurried to the portal, bringing their gifts to the
Infant Christ . . . one carried a goat, another a lamb,
others with loaves of bread, and another a baby's bonnet,
and many other gifts, which they offered with much devotion . . . They continued dancing and singing in their
own language their praises to the Child, asking one another what they had seen and heard and responding with
'Gloria, gloria in excelsis Deo,' and jumping and shout-
ing with much joy."

Here indeed are the basic elements of *Los Pastores,* for
many extant versions in New Mexico have in them the
(1) Annunciation of the birth by the Messiah by an Angel,
(2) the Singing of the Gloria, (3) the Journey to the Manger
at Bethlehem, by the shepherds with their pastoral trappings,
and (4) the impressive and evidently traditional gift-offerings,
or what is better known as 'the Adoration Scene.'

Padre Fray Alonso de Ponce continues his narration, thus:

". . . Then arrived the Kings, guided by a star of
tinsel which they moved ingeniously by cords placed on
pulleys, one on the hill, the other on the door of the
church. When the Kings arrived at the church, the star

disappeared . . . Soon the Kings came into the presence of King Herod, who called together certain wise men who searched in a big book the prophecy concerning the coming of the promised Messiah . . . Finally he gave them permission to go and find the Christ Child and adore Him . . . The star appeared again on the scene, and this light guided the Kings until they arrived at the *portal de Belén,* where postrating themselves they offered baskets of gifts made of silver to the Divine Infant . . ."

It is not possible to state with any degree of certainty the exact period when the religious drama in New Mexico passed from the Church to the Folk. This transition probably began rather early, perhaps in the first part of the De Vargas period of re-colonization. In the century after the reconquest, missions and towns were scattered over wide areas, so that the missionary *padres* found it difficult to minister regularly to both Indian missions and the parishes of the Spanish-colonials.

And left to themselves, the Spanish people, many of whom were the hardy descendants of Oñate, or De Vargas and his *reconquistadores,* took their religion into their homes with their carved *santos* and their homemade *nacimiento*-scenes. They also took their religious plays into the folk-memory, and taught them by repetition and word of mouth to the younger members in each community. The missionary *padres* must have been very proud that these pioneers were passing on to younger generations the very best of their indo-european Christian culture.

Soon after, in the event that the few missionaries still left scattered throughout New Mexico could not be present for Midnight Mass, at other than the more important centers of population, in certain mountain hamlets and villages, the people staged the performance of their particular version of *Los Pastores.* These performances, under the direction of the people themselves, took place in the village church or *placita,* or maybe in a neighbor's large *sala,* graciously loaned for that purpose. Usually a *nacimiento,* similar to that arranged by the immortal Saint Francis of Assisi in faraway Greccio, would be placed as a central setting. Candles would light up the *sala* for the big event, and a huge fire in the fireplace kept everyone cozy and warm during the long performances, while outside, *luminarias* lighted the way for late-comers.

Eventually in the small towns and villages of New Mexico, families or interested groups of villagers began to vie with one another for the privilege of directing the plays or participating in them in coveted roles. Particular roles sometimes passed from father to son, for generations, even to our own time. By the 19th century, a few groups developed an interesting version, and going from town to town presented a repertoire of Christmas mystery plays.

For example, one group's repertoire might include such plays as *Adan y Eva, El Coloquio de los Pastores, Las Apariciones de Nuestra Señora de Guadalupe, El Niño Perdido,* and end up with the last in the series, entitled *Los Reyes Magos.* Today, however, most of the folk troupes remain in their general locale, vying only with the closest village-neighbors with a play-version that they consider strictly their own, and perhaps boasting of the finest Lucifer (one of the Devils) ; for this role is usually the most coveted in *Los Pastores,* requiring great versatility.

Folklorists, artists, writers and the great majority of contented New Mexicans recognize the strong influence exerted by the Franciscan spirit in the Southwest. Manners, customs, life itself throughout the length and breadth of the state are impregnated with this major contributing factor toward the existence and preservation of these medieval morality plays of centuries ago. Simplicity is the keynote of this unique art.

There is still another characteristic associated with the land, which is also a contributing factor to the survival of these mystery pageants, and that is the awe-inspiring beauty of New Mexico, a natural quality which is conducive to thought and meditation. This beauty impresses poor and rich alike, the learned and the unlettered enjoy its presence all around us. It fascinates artists and lures countless writers to our midst. The land is indeed a natural setting for the drama of life, and the dramatization of religion. Its effect upon visitors may be gleaned from the impressions of D. H. Lawrence, on his first visit to the land of "sun, silence, and adobe:"

". . . the moment I saw the brilliant, proud morning sun shine high up over the desert of Santa Fe, something stood still in my soul, and I started to attend . . . for a greatness of beauty I have never experienced anything like New Mexico."

Christmas Eve in Santa Fe

If we would find ourselves with them
Who came that night to Bethlehem,
This coming near is easier far
Here in the hills where the silences are—
Not in the city's glare and roar,
But here where much is as before—
Where the snow-filled ruts of the winding street
Are a path for memory's retreat
To that far-off time in a far-off place
Where the world first saw the Christ-child face.
These long low homes of sun-baked clay
Are simple as stable where He lay;
And the watchful hills in their silent ring
Seem waiting to hear the angels sing.
From the church's door the streaming glow
Touches with gold the falling snow
And shows the darkened figures pass
Within to welcome of midnight Mass.
Welcome is bright along the ways
In the piñon fires' fragrant blaze
And paper sacks with their candle glow
Along the house-tops in ordered row.
It truly is Christmas Eve, we know,
Where the lines of farolitos glow
And luminarias light the snow.

                              —Roland English Hartley

(Reprinted courtesy New Mexico Magazine)

CHAPTER 6

Excerpts from Los Pastores

The clash of swords brings the crowd to its feet. The shepherds step back to make room for their champion, the young man in silver armor, wearing large stiff wings. The swordsmen pause, engage in loud, violent arguments, then fly at each other again. The man in the black mask, red costume and long tail, is cunning and powerful, yet a clean thrust from the silver sword downs him. But even as the victor stands, sword upraised in triumph, his heel upon the vanquished devil, the black-hooded man leers evily at the attentive audience.

This is the climax of *Los Pastores,* the triumph of the Archangel Michael over his satanic majesty Lucifer. Then will follow the touching adoration scene, when all the shepherds and the shepherdess, the hermit and even lazy Bartolo hastened to adore the Christ Child at the manger.

A performance of *Los Pastores,* the Shepherd's Play, is a fascinating medieval experience. But to an outsider, especially those of us Americans who do not have the cultural background to appreciate the many nuances of meaning, both the serious and comical sallies that constantly go on between the varied characters in the play, there is only one suggestion that should be heeded. To really enjoy *Los Pastores* it is necessary to understand the true meaning of the drama's title: it is called in Spanish *El Coloquio de Los Pastores,* which translates literally into English as The Dialogue of the Shepherds. It is a simple folk interpretation of the probable reaction of the Shepherds, and the atmosphere with which the birth of the Messiah was impregnated; it is a harmonious blending of the prophecies that preceded the Coming of Christ, the scriptural background behind the story of our redemption, and the human and comic elements that comprise human nature everywhere. While the original 'Shepherds' Play' was devised in Spain many centuries ago, in Mexico it gathered choice New World flavoring, and in New Mexico, it has evolved into charming folklore.

Here is a summarized version of one of the *coloquios;* and the story is pretty much the same in any other version, except perhaps in the archaic names of the shepherds themselves. If invited to attend a performance, especially if portrayed in such authentic atmosphere and surroundings as *el Santuario de Chimayó,* or at the mission-church of the village of Trampas, review quickly the following resumé, and you will enjoy the play on words, both serious and comical, throughout the drama. Where the archaic Spanish is beyond facile comprehension, watch the action carefully, and sooner or later you will get into the mood of the production.

The Story of the Shepherds

The Archangel Michael appears to the shepherds and tells them of the marriage of Joseph and Mary, prophesying that She will bear the Messiah. Lucifer is disconcerted by the news that a virgin will bear a child and consults with his henchman, Asmodeus, who agrees that such a happening is impossible. The Archangel Michael, however, refutes them and reaffirms the news of the forthcoming birth. Lucifer is perturbed, and when Asmodeus belittles his fears, Lucifer asserts that for God nothing is impossible.

Danteo, one of the shepherds, leaves for Jerusalem to verify the news announced by the angel. A shepherd prepares the flocks for the night and then sings the other fellow-shepherds to sleep. Lucifer then appears, telling the vigilant-night watchman that he is Danteo, who has become sunburned on his journey. The shepherd does not believe him and refuses his embrace, saying that he smells like fireworks. The watchman arouses the other shepherds to tell them he has seen the Devil, and each expresses his abhorrence. The hermit exorcises Lucifer.

Danteo returns from Jerusalem but insists that the shepherds dance before he relates his news. They do so, and the hermit enjoys this activity immensely. Danteo then tells in detail the divine selection of Joseph as Mary's husband and the events leading up to their marriage. He sings for the shepherds the verses which the angels sang to Joseph and Mary when they were married. Lucifer hears Danteo's story and is naturally exceedingly angry.

The following morning the shepherds gather their flocks and leave for Bethlehem. At nightfall they make camp, and Gila (the shepherdess) prepares the meal from each shepherd's contribution of food. The hermit, however, brings only a few herbs, and Gila scorns them. Lucifer appears to the hermit and attempts to gain his favor by sympathizing with him, but the hermit rebukes him and hastens to the shepherds to relate what he has seen. The shepherd-watchman says that it is all a ruse by which the hermit hopes to gain food and advises the hermit mockingly to spend his time praying. Lucifer is angry because he cannot convert the hermit, yet he offers him aid if he will turn against the shepherds. Lucifer then berates the hermit, accusing him of cultivating the shepherd's friendship so that he may increase his own flocks. The hermit and the shepherd-watchman both refuse Lucifer's support, and therefore Lucifer threatens to destroy them with thunderbolts. The Archangel Michael intervenes to prevent Lucifer from carrying out his plan. He complains to Michael that God's granting redemption to man is unfair. Lucifer threatens war upon Michael, who announces that God has sent him to vanquish Lucifer. After several long rhetorical speeches, they do battle, and Michael easily defeats Lucifer. Michael then bids the shepherds to continue their journey to Bethlehem.

The shepherds arrive at the manger in Bethlehem, where each one greets Mary and the Child Jesus with much praise and humble simplicity. In pairs they approach the manger to offer gifts to the Infant Jesus. Each one has something special to offer the Christ Child, and in colorful verse adores the Messiah, presents his gifts and moves back to his place near the entrance. Even Bartolo — who personifies human sloth —

goes up to present his personal gift, but only after having been begged and pushed and coaxed and finally threatened with a whipping. Finally one of the shepherds persuades Gila to arrange for the singing of a special lullaby, and the shepherdess, assisted by three or four shepherds, places the Christ Child in a blanket, and gently sings the Christ Child to sleep. After begging special blessings for their families and their flocks, the shepherds return home, but now filled with an extraordinary joy and peace of mind and heart for which they are ever so grateful.

Excerpts from Los Pastores

SCENE I:
Some fields southeast of the town of Bethlehem.

THE TIME:
Christmas Eve, December 24th, in the evening.

PRELUDE: SCENE I:
The Shepherds are in the fields, quietly keeping watch over their flocks. Some of the shepherds are standing, while others are reclining on the ground.

TEBANO:
"What a beautiful night! . . . All is calm and tranquil . . . Like that must have been the first night, when God created the world. What magnificent stars, so resplendent . . . Friends, let us sing something in praise of the Lord, who made all this for our benefit!"

NABAL:
"What will we sing, *amigos?* King David's song: 'The Lord is the earth'?" (Psalm 23)

PARRADO:
"No, no, it is too long and sad. We need something more cheerful, something that will refer to the promised Messiah."

45

TEBANO:

"Then, let us sing the song of the beautiful bird called *el jilguero* (the linnet)."

BARTOLO:

"That is the one. I like it because it's something peppy, which will shake off some of my laziness."

TEBANO:

"*Jilguero,* how sweetly dost thou sing,
With the sweet voice of a clarion:
Go, wake up the souls,
For it is not time to sleep, now.

CHORUS:

"Ah! How beautiful is the night,
When Jesus was born,
And the Angels sang along,
Until it was nearly dawn."

PARRADO:

"To all the world new Light,
But where shall I find,
This Messiah so promised? . . .
To whom shall I turn and ask
The way which leads to Bethlehem? . . .

CHORUS:

"Shepherd, do not be sad,
And do not torment yourself,
Because the stars will guide you,
To see the newly born . . .

SCENE II:

THE ANGEL:

"Shepherds of these mountains,
Please do not be afraid,
Hear my voice, listen to my words,
I come to announce to you,
News of the greatest joy,
Which the world has had
For long ages: CHRIST IS BORN!
The Light of our souls,

He, who is the fountain of life,
And the source of great joy!

ALL THE SHEPHERDS:

"Tell us where He is.
O heavenly messenger!"

THE ANGEL:

"In Bethlehem He is born,
Amongst humble straw,
In a little rustic shelter,
There in the Sacred City.

THE HERMIT:

"I also heard a song like yours,
Coming from the Orient."

THE ANGEL:

"Shepherds, who in the shelters,
Keep watch over your flocks,
Go ye on to Bethlehem,
Because the WORD WAS MADE FLESH!

CHORUS:

"Glory to God in the Highest,
And peace to men on earth,
Because in the shelter resides,
The Sacred Omnipotence!"

SCENE III:

GILA, THE SHEPHERDESS:

"Shepherds, the day has arrived,
When we will all be marching,
To the shelter of Bethlehem,
To see a happy miracle.
So, arrange well all your canteens,
And also get ready your provisions,
And then we will go with pleasure,
Without much loss of time."

SONGS AND MARCHES:

TWO SHEPHERDS:

With the joyful songs, let us march happily,
Especially those sung by nightingales . . ."

CHORUS:

> "Let us travel happily, Brother Shepherds,
> That we may soon see the Messiah,
> Who doth lie on straw in Bethlehem..."

NARRATIVE:

The Shepherds start marching towards Bethlehem, where they expect to see the Messiah lying in a manger. On their journey towards Bethlehem, they sing pastoral songs of joy, joining nature with all its inherent beauty, in praising God in their simple shepherd fashion.

Stopping on their journey to the manger, they ask Gila, the shepherdess, to fix supper for they are very hungry. They all unpack their provisions, and bring out the *tamales* to be warmed up on the fire. The Hermit, while supper is being prepared, seeks a cave so that he can pray without being molested, while the tired shepherds recline on the cold ground, as they patiently await suppertime.

SCENE V

LUCIFER:

> "On the slope of that wooded mountain,
> I see some shepherds coming...
> I am Lucifer, and there is light abundant in me,
> Light is seen in my name...
> Tremble, heavenly mansions,
> Tremble, you wretched world,
> Because if I am thy hated rival,
> Remember, I can do thee eternal harm...."

CHORUS:

> "From the celestial empire,
> Lucifer, indeed, has fallen ignominiously,
> Only because he pretended,
> To induce the angels into sin..."

NARRATIVE:

In a hellish rage, Lucifer, in a long-winded and fiery speech condemns himself for having been so proud, as to have lost even heaven itself. He tells the shepherds that hell is terrible, that he is downright miserable, and that everyone shall suffer and be wretched like he is. After discoursing all about the wonderful creation of the world, he praises God in simple justice, and he pities himself, and then proceeds to tell the scriptural story of the promised Messiah.

CHORUS:
> "For he was born for our good,
> The King of the infinite Heaven!
> A Virgin, pure and chaste,
> Has given Him birth in Bethlehem!"

LUCIFER:
His many evil cohorts come out to accompany their hellish leader. Satan, another important devil, then proceeds to hand Lucifer a book, and Lucifer proceeds to read to all his companions that the prophecies are all too clear as to the promised birth of the Messiah.

THE FINALE:
Evil has finally been defeated by Good! Lucifer has been vanquished by the Archangel Michael. The Shepherds are now ready to proceed peacefully to Bethlehem. The City of David is their goal, and they are impatient to get started. Gila, a practical woman, inquires whether everyone has the provisions ready. Each one of the Shepherds has a special gift to present to the Christ Child, and there is a joyful atmosphere in their midst. Everyone is ready to approach the stable where they expect to find the Messiah, everyone except lazy Bartolo, who is just too lazy to get up and get started.

This 'Adoration Scene' is classical in its simplicity, Bartolo represents laziness in the life of every Christian. While the shepherds are amazed at the beauty of the Christ Child, they offer their individual gifts, but they are nonetheless disturbed that one of their number is just too lazy to make the effort. Promises of gifts, special privileges and every imaginable strategy is tried, everything which might have tempted almost any other individual, but still Bartolo is unmoved. Perhaps the following response of the lazy Bartolo best exemplifies his attitude.

MENGO:
> "In Bethlehem, Bartolo, is Glory itself!"
> Good Bartolo, let us go there and adore!"

BARTOLO:

> "If Glory wishes to see me,
> Let Glory come here instead!"

NARRATIVE:

But finally, after much prodding and promises of extravagant gifts and privileges, Bartolo gets ready to approach the manger; the shepherds, fearing a trick, are all very alert and they accompany Bartolo all the way to the crib. All is well with the world! Now the whole cast of *Los Pastores* performs its most touching duty: they will place the Christ Child on a blanket, and will rock Him to sleep with their sweetest lullaby.

PARRADO AND TEBANO:

> "Beautiful Child, oh, how I wish,
> with such great and tender affection,
> To thank You a thousand times,
> For gaining the victory against evil itself . . .

THE CHORUS:

> "Cover me with the cloth of Thy tender love,
> Please come to my soul and stay awhile,
> Do you want me to come closer to the crib,
> And lull you to heavenly sleep? *A la ru, A la ru.*"

Prayer to Saint Francis
At Christmas Time

Francis of Assisi, gentle Saint—
Who loved your brother men,
Who loved all brother creatures—
Francis, Little Brother,
Who loved the Feast of Christmas
And fashioned, long ago, a Christmas manger,
That your brother men and birds and beasts
Might see and live the beautiful story
Of the birth of the little Lord Jesus—
Might join in worship and praise—
Little Brother of us all,
Come, walk the earth once more!
Come, with your eagerness and joy,
To show earth's children how to live
And laugh and sing, in love, together—
Gentle Francis of Assisi,
Come, teach us how to fashion
And keep within each heart
A Christmas manger!

—Dorothy A. Linney

(Reprinted courtesy New Mexico Magazine)

CHAPTER 7

San Francisco y el Nacimiento

Saint Francis Built the First Creche

Santa Fe is indeed the "Royal City of the Holy Faith of St. Francis," and no season of the year bears this truth out more than the Christmas holidays. Many and very striking are the artistic murals depicting the life of *Il Poverelo,* 'the Poor man of Assisi,' in the local Art Museum, and the more recent mural-story-painting of St. Francis can be seen in the spacious entrance hall of the Cathedral Parochial School. School children of all ages, on entering and again when leaving St. Francis school cast interested glances at the magnificent panorama depicted there, and theirs is the pleasure of being familiar with the "Canticle of Creatures," that harmonious blending of life and death, sun and moon, night and day, the epic poem in brilliant color and form.

As regards the extraordinary joy and compassion of St. Francis and the mystery of Christ's birth in Bethlehem, Fray (Brother) Velano, one of the first biographers of the 'Poor Man of Assisi' in the 13th century, gives us this version:

"Leaving Rome, whither he was never to return, Francis set out towards the valley of Rieti. Free from all responsibility now that the Papal Bull of 1222 had given the order of Friars Minor its definitive Statutes, its unique Rule of Religious Life, a new epoch of his life opened before him. He touched the supreme point of his career when, while awaiting death, he only aspired to live quietly in the intimacy of Christ. He reestablished himself it seems, in the hermitage of Fonte Colombo; and as Christmas approached he wished, that year at least, to celebrate it after his own heart."

The humble friary of Fonte Colombo lies a little beyond the Italian village of Greccio, perched high up on a lofty summit, like a jewel in a beautiful setting, standing proudly among the snow-capped rugged rocks of the Italian countryside. Here it was that St. Francis conceived the idea, not only to again commemorate the Nativity of Christ in the usual manner of the faith, but also to re-enact it visually. Was this thing possible, or even allowed liturgically at the same time? Apart from the famous creche scene in the Roman basilica of Santa Maria in Travestere, there was little example for Francis to follow. But Francis believed sincerely that not only could it be done, with permission of the ecclesiastical authorities in Rome, but it certainly should be attempted. Francis, always like an innocent child in his saintly simplicity, felt in his heart the need of making everything vivid and real.

But time was passing rapidly, and the 25th of December was well nigh at hand. There was still much to be done, and in a hurry. Even a suitable location had to be found and arranged. And wasting no time in seeking council and advice concerning this novelty of the liturgy, humble Francis hurried to the Papal Palace to request an audience with Pope Honorious. He explained his plans simply and briefly, and begged the necessary permission to fulfill them. Without a moment's hesitation the Pope gave the 'Poor Man of Assisi' the permission he wanted and sent him home to the Fonte Colombo friary with his blessing.

Therefore, a few days before the Christmas of 1223, while the brothers were busy with their chores, the little Poor Man called to him his good friend, Giovanni Velita, the wealthy and noble Lord of Greccio. This is the man who renounced a brilliant military career to enter Francis' Third Order of Penitence. Opposite Greccio, which stood on a rocky hill on the border of the immense valley, Giovanni possessed a high and pointed mountain, honeycombed with caves and crowned by a small wood. The Saint thought this place was most suitable for the scene to be projected.

"I should like," says Francis to his good friend, Giovanni

Velita, "to celebrate the coming feast of the Savior with you and to commemorate His birth in Bethlehem in such a way as to represent as perfectly as possible the suffering and distress that He endured in His birth and infancy to save us. That is why I want you on this spot to set up a real crib with some hay, with an ox and an ass, like those which held company with the Child Jesus."

Giovanni Velita was very happy to assist in this project, and Francis sent him away recommending him to be diligent so as to have everything ready against his arrival.

The people of the countryside joined the friars of the hermitages round about, bearing torches and candles in the night — that night which like a star has shown down the centuries and will shine forever. By the winding paths of the mountain, the candlelight procession approached the spot where, high up between a great ox and a little ass, the crib was set. It was as bright as noon under the great trees, and rock echoed to rock the psalmody of the friars, mixed with the devout refrains of the crowd. Standing before the crib, filled with compassion and unspeakable joy, the *Poverelo* waited, deeply immersed in silent contemplation.

The news about Francis' project had spread in Greccio like a thief in the night. Everyone was there at the cave with Francis and the friars. The bells of the friary tower had prefaced the procession to the realistic manger-scene, and the night was alive with thousands of flickering candles carried by the villagers and many others from the surrounding countryside. Francis and his brothers had commenced the solemn procession through the village, onward to the cave where the ceremonies were to be held. There in a large cave were lifelike appearances of Mary and Joseph kneeling with eyes fixed on the Child Jesus lying in the manger and wrapped in swaddling clothes.

It was indeed *la Noche Buena* as the Spanish speaking people like to call Christmas Eve. The Mass began at an altar placed in an overhanging niche. The celebrant, Brother Leo, clothed in white vestments of the Christmas season, and Francis vested in the dalmatic as deacon of the Mass, ready to assist. At the correct moment of the Holy Sacrifice of the Mass, Francis took up the Book of the Holy Gospel and sang out the words in a loud clear tone. Then he preached a sermon concerning the birth of the Poor King in the little town of Bethlehem. And often when he would name Jesus Christ, he would call Him 'the Child of Bethlehem.'

"It was thus a marvelous night of nights, and it is not to be wondered at that God willed to pour His benefits on this blessed spot. Many sick persons recovered their health. Domestic animals even were healed by eating some stalks of the hay. It is true that on this hay the Saviour of the World had miraculously lain," wrote Brother Celano.

"Giovanni Velita recounts indeed that the Child Jesus was seen as if asleep there in the rustic crib, and that at a certain moment the Divine Child awoke and opened His eyes to smile at St. Francis."

How then, could the venerable City of Santa Fe — *La Villa Real de la Santa Fe de San Francisco de Asís* — celebrate the joyous season of Christ's Nativity without referring, however briefly, to the popularization of the manger-scene of Bethlehem?

But at Christmas time, St. Francis' popularization of the manger-scene of Christ's birth comes to the fore. On Palace Avenue, across from the hospital, one can see an artistic representation of *San Francisco* with different animals, among them the quaint burro, as if preparing them for a formal visit to the nearest creche-scene in front of the Cathedral. On the roof of the Franciscan Fathers' rectory a parish society depicts St. Francis venerating *el Niño Jesús* in a rustic crib background.

La Fonda, "at the end of the Santa Fe Trail," goes all out to enrich and enhance the joyous Christmas spirit with its terraced and colorful presentation of the yuletide spirit of St. Francis as regards the birth and message of Jesus Christ — the Messiah so long expected! The central figure atop La Fonda Hotel is the immortal *San Francisco de Asís* gazing at the figure of the Christ Child in a crib filled with straw. On either side are figurines depicting both religious orders of men and women established by the famous Precursor of the Renaissance. Below the central group are two other parts of the magnificent tableaux of religious and the common folk, each going with a burning light or an appropriate gift they approach the creche. Above, from a lofty pedestal, as if symbolizing heaven's great gift to mankind, the Virgin Mary stands silently adoring the God-Man, the long promised Messiah.

Saint Francis and the Franciscan Friars and Santa Fe's religious customs are all part and parcel of the Christian faith in the annual celebration of Christmas. The simplicity of the manger scene, within and without our churches, be it a great stone Cathedral in the town's historic Plaza, or one of the parish churches scattered throughout the city, or even a lowly mission chapel in Agua Fria — *la Capilla de San Isidro* — or one of the Indian pueblo mission-churches, such as *San Diego de Tesuque,* in each one of them, the re-enactment of Christ's Birthday is hallowed with simple faith and humble hope and linked together with apostolic love for one's neighbor. And the *nacimiento,* be it ever so lowly or ever so elaborate, represents the real meaning of Christmas: the birth of the Messiah, it means "Emmanuel — God with us!" Both young and old hasten to contemplate — as did the humble St. Francis — the Redeemer, and having adored the Lord Jesus in the rustic crib, they return home filled with the spirit of Mary and Joseph and the simplicity of the lowly shepherds.

And since the Franciscan vision of life begins with Christmas, so Santa Fe tries to emulate the spirit of St. Francis. "Challenging the unforgetfulness of men, Francis on that memorable Christmas night re-enacted before the eyes of his fellow Umbrians the drama of Bethlehem in so simple and unsophisticated a manner that the most unlettered peasant could not fail to comprehend its meaning. With the crib Francis taught the world once again that God had become Emmanuel — God with us." Santa Fe has never forgotten that lesson!

O Ancient Bells, Chime Out

O ancient bells of ancient Santa Fe,
Your metals, fused and cast in far-off lands,
Chime clearly out above the world's melee.

From mingled notes of joy and grief you play
A chorale that triumphantly expands,
O ancient bells of ancient Santa Fe.

So strength and beauty blend in ores and clay,
And strains of song from hills and desert sands,
Chime clearly out above the world's melee.

You ring with vibrant sound while people pray
In diverse tongues to God who understands,
O ancient bells of ancient Santa Fe.

For prayers are songs, and song is prayer that may
Be echoed in each heart till love's commands
Chime clearly out above the world's melee.

While quickened hearts, in tune on Christmas Day,
Are listening, and hands are clasping hands,
O ancient bells, of ancient Santa Fe—
Chime clearly out above the world's melee!

—Dorothy A. Linney

(Reprinted courtesy New Mexico Magazine)

Las Comidas de Navidad

Traditional Foods at Christmas

After a devout attendance at the traditional *Misa del Gallo,* the Cathedral midnight services, my enthusiastic grandparents knew it was then time for a delightful festive meal. It was time to eat! *El señor arzobispo* had delivered an inspiring Christmas *sermoncito,* and he had emphasized that "the Word was made flesh and dwelt amongst us." And the brisk walk home on a cold wintry road had whetted our appetites. To make the Divine Guest (Emmanuel — God with us!) feel at home in our humble abode, *mis abuelitos* felt that there was nothing more soul-satisfying — after one had fulfilled his feastday obligation of attending Mass — than to share and partake of the good food and delicacies at *la fiesta de Navidad.*

Perhaps it is an ingrained prejudice of centuries, but here in northern New Mexico *los platillos nativos* — the native dishes — at Christmas-time seem to be extra delightful and ever more delicious, even to the most discriminating palate. Undoubtedly, it is because of the careful preparations that precede the festive foods to help celebrate *el cumpleaños del Niño Jesús* (Christ's birthday) that make *las comidas de Navidad* that much more appetizing. At any rate, there's nothing better in the Southwest! Permit me to share the atmosphere of those wonderful days, a time not too long ago, when the warm galvanizing influence of my grandparents still held together all the members of our large clan. Those happy memories still influence most of us today.

Any worthwhile cook certainly knows that to prepare a good fiesta meal, the preparations have to be complete, if not elaborate. The Spanish-speaking *Neomejicanos,* to begin with, have always looked forward to *la Noche Buena,* Christmas Eve. It is more than just a special night of the calendar year, or of the winter season. It is 'the Night of nights.' It is a state of mind that harmonizes heart and soul in a festive mood of liturgical worship and family togetherness. Christ the Redeemer came down to our humble earth so that we might live ever more fully "in Him, by Him and for Him." And so, once the heart and the soul had duly rendered the Messiah the worship which is His due, it was now time to celebrate in the family circle, with all the joy which our human nature could muster. It was time for a family *fiesta,* a continuation of that colorful heritage which we received from Spain and Mexico, and which in *Nuevo Méjico* our ancestors had grafted with the best of the Pueblo Indian. Our Christmas meal has developed into something which is not strictly Spanish, nor yet completely Mexican, but rather a combination of the two, with the unmistakable flavoring of the *puebleño,* our Indian neighbors and friends.

In my grandmother's thick-walled adobe home the elaborate *nacimiento* often found its perfect setting in the rather spacious kitchen. Some of the members of the family usually objected, preferring the creche in *el cuarto del recibo,* in the extra orderliness of the living room, but *mi abuelita* was a matriarch in the real sense of the term: in her *casa propria* — her own home! — she supervised everything, and especially at Christmas-time, when so many domestic preparations were in order. So, *los nietos,* her grandchildren, set up the rustic *nacimiento* in a corner of *la cocina,* while grandmother worked hard with the *posole* and the *empanaditas.* Besides, *la rama de pino,* the pine branches, gave off a pleasant odor from the creche, and the titillating aroma in the kitchen gave great promise of a culinary adventure.

Ya habían hecho el pan, the bread-making had already been done days before, an expression which at Christmas-tide meant not only those large loaves of homemade bread, but which now included all those other pastries that were specialties of the season. Only the *sopaipillas* were left for last, so that they would be fresh for after Mass; *tortas grandes,* large loaves of delicious bread, to be eaten in thick slices or broken up in chunks like French bread; and always while baking the Christmas bread, *mi abuela* would complain that if only it were bread made Indian-style, *pan de horno de indio,* the large delightful loaves that only Indians can produce in those beehive ovens. But it was wintertime, and to make up for the Indian-loaves, grandma would prepare extra batches of *molletes,* sweet rolls with anice seed; and, of course, there were always large-sized *pasteles de manzana o de durazno, o de albaricoque,* pies made from the dried *orejón,* dried apples, peaches or apricots. Now we grandchildren remembered the harsh scoldings of summertime, when we would be caught stealing handsful of dried fruit. *El orejón de frutas,* the carefully dried fruit of harvest-time had been prepared with a specific purpose: to regale the family with delicious pies *para la Navidad.*

But Christmas would never be *la Navidad* without plenty of *bizcochitos,* those favorite, mouth-watering and fast-dissolving cookies that defy definition and description. *Bizcochitos* prefer to be enjoyed than to be described! Dozens upon dozens of these inimitable delicious pastries were always necessary, for they were the most popular way to enjoy *vino del país* (native wine) or other store-bought liquers; and, many times during the holiday season, when neighbors would drop in for a chat, there was nothing better than freshly brewed *cafecito* and the delicious munching of *bizcochitos* or *pastelitos de orejón,* little pies.

And yet, if during the holidays *mi abuelita* would offer us a choice between those wonderful-testing *bizcochitos* and her extra rich *empanaditas,* we would be hard put to decide. Personally, I much preferred several samples of each! The delicious turnovers, *las empanaditas,* are definitely a Christmas pastry. It just wouldn't be Christmas without them! Waiting for the licking of the spoons and pans, *los nietos* savoured a bit of everything that was included in the stuffing. *Las empanaditas* were like a treasure-house filled with all kinds of good things to eat. Grandma filled the turnovers with lots of fragrant piñon, those wonderful nuts that we had picked in the autumn and then saved for eating on the cold winter nights near the pot-bellied stove or near *el fogón*, that attractive Indian fireplace. We were fascinated with *la lengua*, the large tongue of beef, that was specially prepared for the stuffing; and in the mincemeat that was the inevitable *orejón de frutas*, the dried fruits which were cooked slowly and which produced an enchanting aroma; and we could hardly wait to taste *las empanaditas* once the first batch was deep-fried and set out to cool. When the turnovers were finished, I can still remember *Mamá Nina* (the affectionate dimunitive we had evolved from Grandma's real name, Doña Catarina) asking us to leave the fragrant *cocina* while she hid a large *olla de hojalata*, a big pail, of *empanaditas* for an emergency during the holidays. We didn't mind leaving the warm kitchen, because sooner or later we would share in those 'extra' turnovers when *amigos y parientes*, friends and relatives, would drop in for a visit.

After attending *la Misa del Gallo*, trudging home in the falling snow, stoking the fire in the old fashioned wood stove, warming one's hands by the warmth of the ready-food, helping set the festive table, all this was the prelude to an unforgettable Christmas dinner. In many homes, our neighbors preferred to wait until noon on Christmas Day, but at *la casa de mis abuelos*, at my grandparents' place, two or three o'clock in the morning, after Midnight Mass, was just as good as any to enjoy the *fiesta* food. The best dishes were set out on the large *mesa*, and candles lighted at the *nacimiento* in the corner and on the holiday table, the flickering glow of candlelight adding a mysterious touch to the stronger light of *la lámpara de aceite*, the coal-oil lamp. When everything was ready, *mi abuelita* would lead our blind grandfather, *Papá Nan* (his real name was Don Román), to the table, direct him to his special place, and request that he say the Christmas blessing. I can still remember clearly that wonderful old man, mellowed by great age and the sorrow of his incapacitating blindness, but alive and alert and ever grateful to Almighty God for the many kindnesses showered upon him by all his large family, young and old. In simple prayer and then with a majestic sign of the cross over the table, he was a perfect picture of the benevolent patriarch of the Spanish-speaking people.

Now it was time to eat! Grandma would quietly pass out steaming bowls of tantalizing *posole,* that delicious homemade hominy blown up to the size of large popcorn, swimming with good boiled beef and pork, and strongly seasoned with *orégano* and colored and flavored with large-sized crimson-red *chile colorado.*

The second course consisted of a generous pie-slice of those double-layered *enchiladas al estilo neomejicano,* not the rolled-up restaurant variety, but the real homemade 'chile pies' made with either wheat flour or corn *tortillas,* and well-structured with lots of redolent onion and flavorful yellow cheese, and covered over with quite coarsely ground red chile from either Chimayó or Santa Cruz. Sidelining the *enchilada* was Spanish-style rice, *arroz á la española,* cooked in olive oil and seasoned tomato sauce. Then were served *los refritos,* those delicious refried pinto beans, adding a familiar taste to the *enchilada. Calabacitas con chicos,* the summer-dried native squash and corn, were placed in a large bowl in the middle of the table, each member of the family partaking of this dish when ready. Steaming freshly brewed *cafecito* filled brimming *tasas,* extra large cups. For the children there were large *vasos de agua,* tumblers filled with ice-cold well water, or large cups of delicious *chocolate de fiesta,* that delightful holiday chocolate drink.

Sparkling conversation centered around the Christmas Mass, and the special sermon of the feastday by the bishop, with news of the many *amigos y parientes,* the friends and relatives, who had been seen at church services and who had promised a formal visit during the Yuletide season. Comments on what a large crowd had filled the *Catedral de San Francisco,* and how charmingly the *nacimiento* had been prepared for the feast of Christ's birth. Almost everybody had stayed a few minutes after Mass to approach the creche *para adorar al Niño Jesús,* to venerate the lifelike image of the Christ Child in the rustic manger. Then the conversation turned to the relatives, and which relations were to be visited by whom, and what *regalo del corazón,* what gift was to be taken to what *pariente.*

With the dinner dishes taken up by the women-folk, eyes lighted up at the sight of the amber-hued *vino del país,* or some other family favorite liquer. And then came the *piece de resistance,* steaming bowls of *sopa,* that delightfully delicious bread pudding that is a must for such an occasion as *la Navidad.* While the young people called it *sopa,* the older people insisted on calling it by another name; they preferred to call it *capirotada;* but whatever named it was called, it was still delectable bread pudding that is a local native specialty. Cinnamon-flavored, and heavily braced with good melted cheese and full of nut-flavored *piñon* and lots of raisins, *sopa* is the best way to finish the festive *comida de Navidad,* a holiday meal which is a unique expression of good cookery. It is the only one of its kind in the world!

When everyone had had their fill of the special Christmas foods, some of the family retired for several hours of well-needed sleep, while the more energetic headed back to the Cathedral to attend several of the countless masses offered on the various altars. At Christmas time each *padre* is allowed the unique privilege of celebrating not only one, but three special Masses. Many Catholics look forward to observing the liturgy of the three Masses, joining the tradition of the Church in its threefold sentiments. Permit me to quote very briefly a resumé of this ancient liturgical tradition:

". . . For the birthday of Our Lord, the Church in her liturgy surrounds the Christ on her altars with the setting of Bethlehem. Each Christmas at the hush of midnight (Midnight Mass), we recall the birth of the Divine Light, come to dispel the darkness of the world. Each Christmas in the still of dawn (the second Mass), we join the shepherds at the crib in adoring Christ in the form of a Babe. Each Christmas at the quiet of the midday sun (the third Mass), we sing the praises of the Saviour of the world, the Word Who was made flesh and dwelt amongst us.

Thus we find in the three Masses of Christmas the idea of the progressive revelation of Christ: in the darkness of the night, the Saviour came, known only to Mary, Joseph and the angels; at the first light of dawn, the shepherds, the few chosen people, found Christ, our Saviour; at the noonday sun, the Saviour of the whole world is revealed to all men."

During the day of Christmas, my grandparents thought it was the most natural thing to expand their largess of festive joy beyond the confines of the family circle. For one thing, the food preparations had entailed much work, and with so much extra food, it was only fitting that it be shared with friends and relatives and neighbors. Just as the shepherds had bestowed humble but sincere gifts on the Holy Family, in honor of the coming of the promised Messiah, gifts which were probably of a pastoral nature — lambs, homemade cheese, skins of milk, and other things that formed part of their shepherd life — so the Spanish-speaking people give and share 'gifts of the heart.' Bowls of homemade pastries were prepared and taken to homes of friends and neighbors. In turn, our family would be regaled with similar gifts. In the name and in honor of *el Niño Jesús,* many in our neighborhood shared with each other their festive fare.

Likewise on Christmas day, groups of neighborhood children would shyly approach my grandparents' home ¡*Vienen a pedir Oremos!* They were coming to let my family share with them some of our favorite Christmas goodies. These *niños* were not beggers. Far from it! At Christmas all children have a legitimate right to ask their elders to share their delicacies and gifts. Christmas is *el cumpleaños del Niño Jesús,* the birthday of the Christ Jesus, and in His name and is His honor it is a privilege for parents and elders to bestow gifts upon their children.

Among the Spanish-speaking, a certain type of dignity permeates *la pedida de los 'Oremos,'* the seeking of holiday gifts. With the simplicity and innocence characteristic of *chiquitos de Dios,* the little ones enjoy Christmas, for it is in a special way their own day. For did not Christ one day say:

"Unless you become as little children, you shall not enter the Kingdom of Heaven?" Thus, in a spirit of devout reverence for Christ's coming to the world as a Babe in the stable of Bethlehem, *los mayores,* the older folks expected the *niños* to recite the quaint ditty that synthesized the spirit of Christmas. Knocking shyly at the door, the *chiquitos* would push the oldest *niño* to the foreground, and they would sing:

Oremus, oremus,	We pray thee, we do pray thee,
Angelitos somos;	Know that we are but angels;
A pedir aguinaldos	And from heaven we've just come,
y rezando oremus.	To beg thee for thy little gifts.

This coming and going of little children with cold hands and wet feet, kept up practically all morning. And in the glad spirit of Christ's birthday, no one was sent away without some little gift, at least of food or pastries. It really didn't matter how few or how many goodies were given out at any one Christmas. What was really important was that each gift of food or pastry or toy was bestowed on *los niños* with light-hearted friendliness and human warmth. And to make *la pedida de los 'Oremus'* ever more interesting, some of the older folks insisted that before they would give a *chiquito* some little gift, the child would first recite the 'Our Father' aloud, and shyly the *niño* would obey.

Among *los neomejicanos,* the proverbial saying *Mi casa es suya* is not just one more cute saying of half-hearted hospitality. Actually, it is a unique way of life, a Christian attitude that can mean much more than "Go ahead, make yourself at home!" Call it Old World manners or local native courtesy, or whatever you will. The Latin temperament demands an innate courtesy that knows no bounds, except being foolishly extravagant. Especially at Christmas-time does this gracious sense of Christian hospitality come to the fore, as if it is a studied renewal and determination to practice 'good manners' all the year long.

The following recipes are hereby offered, not because we feel that only we Spanish-speaking people have the best in the world, but rather in the spirit of good friendly neighborliness, we want to share our treasures with everybody around us. It is a 'gift from the heart,' or perhaps better still a fulfillment of that proverb which insists that *"con panza llena, el corazón contento,"* 'there's nothing better than a full stomach!'

TAMALES

Filling enough for 4 dozen tamales.
4 lbs. pork shoulder
6 tbsp. chile powder
6 c. water

Cook meat in 6 c. of water until tender. Remove meat from broth saving broth for dough. Chop meat in ¼ inch pieces and place in pan. Dissolve 6 tblsps. chile powder in 1½ c. of broth, add to meat and cook until almost dry. Set aside while preparing dough (*masa*)

Tamale Dough *masa* for 4 dozen tamales.
5 cups ready mix white corn meal
3 tablespoons pure lard
Remainder of broth from meat
1 pound cry corn husks
PREPARE AND COOK AS FOLLOWS:

Open and clean corn husks *hojas,* trim at both ends. Soak husks in warm water for at least ½ hour. Husks should be about 4 inches wide and 7 inches long before folding. Add pure lard to corn meal, add broth and mix by hand making a medium soft dough. Dough must be of consistency to spread.

Spread dough ¼ inch thick over entire 4 inch width to 3½ inches from top, allowing 3½ inches for fold at bottom. Spread heaping teaspoonful tamale filling down center on dough. Double fold at width, fold overlapping loose end. Place in steamer and steam for an hour, taking care that the tamales do not become soggy.

POSOLE

Hominy Stew — 12 servings:
3 lbs. pork shoulder (cut in chunks)
6 c. water
4 red chile pods, or 3 tblsps. chile powder
½ tsp. oregano
1 small onion
1 clove of garlic, minced
6 c. of canned or frozen hominy

Boil meat until tender in the 6 c. of water. Add hominy, oregano, onion, garlic and chile to boiled meat and broth. Salt to taste. Simmer hominy and meat together for another ½ hour. If frozen hominy is used, cover with water and boil about 6 hours before adding to other ingredients.

ENCHILADAS

For one enchilada:
2 corn tortillas. Enough chile to cover both layers of tortillas for as many as you wish to make.

Dip tortillas in deep fat or skillet with about ¼ inch melted shortening. Do not allow to get crisp. Sprinkle first layer with grated cheese and minced onion. Add layer of chile sauce. Place another fried tortilla on top, cover with chile sauce and again sprinkle with grated cheese and onion. Place enchilada in oven for 5 minutes to melt cheese.

CHILE SAUCE

2 tbsps. shortening
1 tbsp. flour
½ can tomato sauce
6 tbsps. red chile powder
2 c. water

Melt shortening, add flour and brown. Mix tomato sauce, water and chile and add to browned flour. Cook for 10 minutes. Salt to taste and add water if too thick.

CAPIROTADA

Bread pudding — 6 servings.
1 c. sugar
2 c. water
6 slices toasted bread
1 tsp. cinnamon
1½ c. grated or sliced cheese
1 c. raisins
2 tsp. fat

Caramelize sugar. Add water and cinnamon and boil until sugar is dissolved. Place a layer of bread in a casserole. Add cheese and raisins. Repeat until all ingredients are used. Pour syrup over mixture, add fat and bake in a moderate oven until the syrup is absorbed by the bread.

67

EMPANADITAS

Fried Pies — This recipe makes 8 dozen.

Filling: (should be prepared the day before for better flavor)

2 lbs. of cooked beef, or	½ tsp. allspice
1 lb. beef and 1 lb. pork.	1 tsp. nutmeg
2 c. prepared mince meat	¾ c. sugar
½ c. piñon nuts (if not available	1 tsp. salt
substitute pecans. Use pecans	
chopped, piñon nuts whole.)	

Boil meat until tender, cool and grind fine. Add mince meat, spices, nuts and sugar until filling becomes thick and moist. If filling is too dry add a little dark corn syrup.

Dough *masa*:

½ package yeast	1 egg (optional)
3 c. lukewarm water	4 tbsps. pure lard
1½ tbsp. sugar	6 c. flour
1½ tsp. salt	

Place yeast, sugar, salt in mixing bowl, add water, mix until dissolved. Add beaten egg and melted lard adding enough flour for a dry dough. Roll out dough ⅛ inch thick, cut with round cookie cutter about three inches in diameter. Place 1 heaping teaspoon of filling in center of pattie. Fold over and pinch edges together so empanadita dough will seal filling. Trim with pie cutter and deep fry until golden browɳ.

BISCOCHITOS

This recipe makes about 10 dozen small cookies. They taste better if made a few days ahead of time.

1½ c. pure lard	6 c. sifted flour
¾ c. sugar	3 tsp. baking powder
2 egg yolks (optional)	½ c. water
1 tsp. anis seed	1 tsp. salt

Cream sugar and lard until light and fluffy, add anis seed and beaten egg yolks beating for a few seconds. Sift flour, baking powder and salt together, add to mixture. Add water and knead until well mixed. Roll out, cut with fancy cookie cutter and sprinkle with a mixture of sugar and cinnamon. Bake in 350° oven, 12 minutes or until golden brown.

NEW MEXICO CHOCOLATE

This recipe makes 4 cups.

1 quart milk	1 tsp. cinnamon
½ cup sugar	1 pinch salt
4 tbsp. cocoa	

Heat milk to almost boiling point. Mix sugar, cocoa, cinnamon and salt. Add to heated milk.

Christmas In New Mexico

In sleepy little villages that cling to long ago,
The Christmas spirit leads the way in Old New Mexico
Luminarias are gleaming and their silent greetings vie
With beck'ning bonfire fingers blending with the starlit sky;
In the city, shoppers hurry, presents pile and trees are bright—
Kiddies search the clouds for reindeer and their notes
    to Santa write.
How quickly falls the Christmas eve—with midnight
    drawing near—
And as the chimes strike twelve o'clock and carols
    ring out clear,
In silent reverie, we see another midnight when
A Babe in swaddling clothes was King—and kings
    were only men—
We know He walks among us, though He treads on
    silent feet
Over sleepy town and prairie and on busy city street,
On mountain tops where snow hangs heavy on the
    spruce and pine,
And on rocky roads and canyons where the wandering
    rivers wind;
Oh, the Spirit of the Yuletide wanders here on earth again,
Whispering a "Merry Christmas, Peace on Earth,
    Goodwill to Men!"

—Lorna Baker

(Reprinted courtesy New Mexico Magazine)

Los Indios y La Navidad

The Indian Celebration of Christmas

It is Christmas Eve, *la Noche Buena,* and up and down the Rio Grande and the bleak, wintry hills, there is to be found a melange of the haunting unbroken rhythm of the Indian drums and the cry of the Spanish fiddles. It is the peaceful quiet and the solemnity of His presence in time-tattered venerable mission-churches and village chapels. Huge, high carved doors, a treasured craftmanship of Spanish and Indian pioneers, admit both native and visitor inside the sacred precincts. Pot bellied stoves glow red in the shadowy churches, and someone has been charged with the responsibility to keep enough firewood handy for the long midnight services. On the altars, candles set in massive holders send their weird dancing reflections onto the two-foot thick adobe walls which had been carefully whitewashed only the summer before.

Where it is convenient, the Spanish speaking *nativos* hasten to join their neighboring Indian *amigos* to help them celebrate the wonderful mysteries of Christ's birthday. Here in the Indian mission-churches *los neomejicanos* feel perfectly at home, for they reabsorb a cultural flavor which united both *conquistador* and *indio* centuries ago, and which today serves to dramatize the uniqueness of yuletide celebration of Christmas in the Southwest. The Indian emphasis on dancing to express joy on the occasion of *el cumpleaños del Niño Jesús* is but a unique complement to those other dramatic Spanish traditions of *Los Pastores* or *Las Posadas.* The New World provided both Spaniard and Indian the wonderful opportunity to blend harmoniously the best and most interesting of both cultures. Here in northern New Mexico, to separate the colorful and dramatic indo-hispanic flavor of Christmas is to rob both the Spanish-speaking people and the Pueblo Indian of a heritage which is their greatest spiritual treasure.

Let history speak for itself: let us consider the interesting background which explains the fascinating and realistic 'baptism' of the traditional Indian dancing with the Old World Christianity as taught by zealous Franciscan Padres. Old Mexico is the connecting link, for what the missionaries learned in *la Nueva España,* those lessons and experiences were to be duplicated in the far-off 'ancient Kingdom of the New Mexico.' Without belaboring the point, let us content ourselves with the authority of at least one renowned missionary-historian, Padre Fray Toribio de Benavente, that Franciscan who preferred to be called simply *Motolinía* (the Poor Man):

"The Indians celebrate the feasts of the Lord, of Our Lady and of the principal Patron Saints of the towns with more rejoicing and solemnity . . . Attired in white shirts and mantles and bedecked in feathers . . . the Indian lords and chiefs perform dances and sing in their language the songs that solemnize the feast which they are celebrating.

The songs and dances are graceful and harmonious. In many places the dancing and singing begin at midnight, and numerous fires illumine the patios . . . After divine services the Indians sing a great part of the day, and this does not cause them much trouble or inconvenience . . . Generally, the Indians sing, beat drums and ring bells . . .

On Christmas night, the Indians come to the divine services and attend three Masses. Those who cannot find a place in the church, do not for this reason depart. Instead, gathered before the church door and in the patio, and they pray and act as if they were in the church . . ."

Four centuries later, here in New Mexico, we find that same spirit of reverence and joy in the Indian celebration of Christmas. Both native and visitor to pueblo land is hard put to decide just what particular Indian village he will choose in which to enjoy this unique Christmas dancing. The Spanish-speaking person usually prefers the closest neighboring *pueblo* mission-church, for Christmas is to thè *nativo* a challenge to good neighborliness. But whatever *pueblo* is chosen, this truly American celebration of Christ's birthday is soul-satisfying. In no other place in the United States will you see and enjoy and savour centuries-old pageantry in such authentic settings.

On Christmas Eve — on this 'the Good and Wonderful Night of Nights' — midnight Mass in the impressive mission churches is usually followed by colorful ceremonial dances, sometimes performed in the church itself, and sometimes in the *pueblo plaza.* Flaming torches (the *achones* devised by the Indians in Old Mexico in the 16th century and still used by the Taos Indians in the 20th century!) and brightly lit *luminarias* or *hogueras,* those cheery bonfires, all these forms of warmth and lighting illuminate the shadowy *pueblos* as the Indian dancers move in graceful unison to the haunting rhythm of ancient drums. Every once in a while, rifles are fired in noisy salute into the chilly December air, the sharp report happily heralding the long-awaited birth of the Messiah.

For many people, Taos Pueblo serves as a veritable magnet on *la Noche Buena.* What with the impressive adobe-buildings set hard against the magnificently rugged Blue Mountains in the background, with shepherds' fires illuminating the ancient *plaza,* and countless Indian villagers appearing, warmly wrapped, on the terraced roofs awaiting the official command of the pueblo's governor. The whole scene is reminiscent of an elaborate backdrop of a Biblical scene.

Visitors to Taos Pueblo, or to any other *pueblo* for that matter, should always make it a point to stop by the governor's home and inquire just what ceremonies and dances are planned for the particular night. Not only will the Indians tender their characteristic hospitality in finer fashion, but the visitors will be given a better vantage point to enjoy the pageantry. Good manners are especially welcome at Christmas!

Perhaps a few brief quotes from an article entitled GUEST OF THE PUEBLOS, written by a Jemez *puebleño,* Joe Sando, might be most appropriate here:

". . . To non-Indians accustomed to planning months ahead of time for an event, one may be astonished to learn that a big affair like the Indian *fiesta* is possible without advertising, discussion of budgets, and numerous committee meetings. All these are eliminated by the Indians through years of experience as showmen. The Indians have been putting on these *fiestas* since the 16th century when the *conquistadores* assigned each of the *pueblos* a patron saint . . .

It is in honor of the saints that the dances are performed. No budget is required, since there is no purchasing of dance costumes, which are handwoven and handmade by the Indians themselves. Neither do the dances demand remuneration. Committees are uncalled for, since most members of the villages habitually take part in the program in which they are most capable, that is, in dancing or in singing or in beating of the drums."

As the hour of midnight approaches visitors grow apprehensive that the ceremonies won't start on time, while the reserved *puebleños* portray an inner calm and patience that is quite disarming. But authority must be obeyed and respected, and it is up to the governor to give the official command. Family groups stand quietly beside the doors of their adobe apartments, their eyes fastened on the highest roof where the *señor gobernador* will appear shortly. And the head officer of the Indian *pueblo* is indeed a handsome figure, broad shoulders clothed in a brilliant ceremonial blanket, his straight black hair glistening in the light of the fires on the rooftops, and in an impelling voice gravely and solemnly announces: "Come, my people, come to the church for the midnight services!" And to make his command ever more official and dignified, he raises aloft the two canes of *pueblo* authority, the gold-topped cane that denotes authority from Spanish-colonial times and the silver-topped cane that is the Indians' heritage from Abraham Lincoln's days at Washington.

Immediately, the silent and reverent *puebleños* begin to descend from their rooftops and march quietly to the mission church. Everyone who can possibly walk is on his way to *la*

Misa del Gallo, the traditional midnight Mass that the Spanish *padres* introduced with the teachings of Christianity. Inside the venerable adobe mission walls, flickering candlelight illumines the untroubled countenances of a peaceful and religious congregation. And as if keeping faith with traditions that are meant of their very nature to be passed on to countless generations, the *sermoncito de la fiesta de Navidad* will undoubtedly be in Spanish. The lilting beauty of the *idioma español,* with its inherent rhythm and music harmonizes splendidly with the tradition of the Indian which unites ceremonial music and dancing as a unique way of life.

Many people might possibly wonder why there is no contradiction, in the Spanish-speaking mind, with liturgical worship such as the mass and the Indian custom of ceremonial dancing. At first glance, there might be an apparent contradiction, since in the present-day worship of the Spanish-speaking there is no specific time for ceremonial dancing in liturgical worship. But traditions die hard, and sometimes traces of centuries-old customs never really disappear. And then, temperament plays an important part in people's lives.

The Spaniards have always loved dancing, and to find their thousands of neophytes in the New World addicted to ceremonial dancing probably made their Spanish hearts feel good. The *padres* undoubtedly felt very much like the African adventurer Livingstone when he was asked by a native who belonged to some interior tribe in the Dark Continent: "What do YOU dance?" What the African meant by his question was that, a man dances to portray his tribe, his social customs, his religion; for as an anthropologist has put it, "an aborigine does not preach his religion, he dances it."

Thus the Spanish *padres* were obliged to study carefully the countless tribes in Old Mexico before they could effectively start preaching Christianity. Assuredly, some of the *padres* must have remembered seeing ritualistic dancing in Seville, the famous *Danza de los Seises,* that ancient festival ritual dancing that was a specialty on certain feastdays in the Cathedral of Seville. Or perhaps some of the missionaries had heard or seen, on their way to the New World, at Mallorca, on the festival of St. Roch, patron saint of the town of Alaro, young men dance in the church in fanciful costumes with tambourines, up to the steps of the high altar, immediately after Mass, and then dance out of the church. At any rate, the Spaniards with their inherent love of the dance, had found peoples in the *Nuevo Mundo* who insisted on dancing out their religious worship, the Indians who from time immemorial had at one and the same time both worshipped and danced. The *Españoles* in the New World soon found a way to graft upon the rituals of Christian worship the best of ceremonial dancing that their new brothers-in-the-faith loved so much.

That this was an effective 'baptism' of customs from the pagan mentality to the neophyte Christian is evident from Fray Toribio de Motolinía's casual report: "The Indians celebrate the feastdays . . . with much rejoicing and solemnity . . . attired in white shirts and mantles and bedecked in feathers . . . the Indian lords and chiefs perform a dance and sing in their language the songs that solemnize the feast which they are celebrating."

A few years ago an unusually talented Greek visitor came especially to Taos to study the Indian ceremonial dancing. This man, Vassos Kanellos, former art director of the Institute of the Dance in Athens, Greece made a special study of Taos Indian dancing and compared it to ancient Greek rites. His interpretation of the Christmas Eve *Los Matachines* dance is especially interesting here and now, in that an outsider's report is considered to be somewhat objective, and usually a visitor notices many things which familiarity might have caused us to depreciate.

Like most everyone else who sees magnificent Taos the first time, the landscape captivated the Greek visitor from the start. The altitude and the pure air to be breathed in deeply, the natural beauty of the mountains and the wide sagebrush plains, the majestic blue mountain peaks and the ethereal heights, all these things combined to make the Greek visitor and student of Indian dancing closer to things eternal. And he rightly concluded that the Taos Indians, who have dwelt here for many centuries and who have been persistent in keeping both their life and their art tradition pure, have indeed been an inspiration to artists and writers who visit them. As danced in Taos on *la Noche Buena, Los Matachines* is a fascinating ritualistic pageant. Based on a medieval Spanish mystery play, whose origin is presumably lost in history, the New Mexico version is Aztec in spirit, and the actors portray, among other themes, the betrayal of Montezuma by the Spaniards. The title itself implies clowning or mischief-making, and can be compared favorably with the old satyrs of the primitive rituals of Bacchus or Dionysus. As an idea it undoubtedly can be traced back to old Hellas, where even today, the Greek people believe in the evil spirits, the KALIKANTZAROI, or mischief makers, much like the Taos Pueblo Indians believe in today. All through history from pagan times to ours, the Christian religion inherited and adopted characters and types of this order, and these rituals traveled slowly from the Orient to Greece, into Italy, then into Spain, and from the Iberian peninsula into the New World.

It is to the credit of the pueblo Indian who has preserved what he considered best from the Spaniard, that on adopting such an interesting ritual, the Indian enriched it with his own indigenous traditions and developed the dance of *Los Matachines* into a beautiful and artistic spectacle — the paganism which is inspired from Nature, and perhaps with the determined prodding of some zealous *padre* added to it our Christian symbolism.

Los Matachines is usually danced after vesper-services in the mission chapel of St. Francis of Taos early on Christmas Eve. This interesting ritual is danced in honor of the Madonna, whose image is carried by four stalwart Indians wrapped in colorful togas. Before the procession leaves the chapel, several young Indians hurriedly leave the congregation to properly light the *achones,* tall torches of wired cedar and pine fagots, outside the churchyard; these torches will be carried solemnly throughout the procession while the dancers perform their sacred ritual. Rifle-shots serve as the signals for the Indians to fall into a double line behind the statue of the Madonna. *Luminarias,* the shepherd fires, arranged all around the *pueblo* flare into cheery light and invited warmth.

Moving slowly and orderly, the candle-lighted procession serves as a movable-stage for *Los Matachines*. The dancers represent the Twelve Apostles who perform the ritual to a lively melody coming from two musicians, one with a guitar, another with a violin. Dancing a simple but technical combination of steps, in practiced series, the Indians become completely absorbed in prayerful worship. Symbolically, the dancers periodically face each other, holding high the symbol of the Trinity, in the left hand, while the right hand is wrapped in a colorful handkerchief with coins inside. Attentive to the music, the Indians raise the Trinity symbol on high as the coins are rattled noisily. While the coins symbolize material power, the three-united sticks represent the Blessed Trinity, or the power and spirit of the Creator of the Universe.

Enlivening the solemn ritualistic dance are two jesters or clowns, and these are the *abuelo* and the *abuela*. The male clown is suitably dressed up with a head-dress of cowhide and a horrible set of teeth. He carries a menancing whip and directs the dance as if he were the manager of the production. The female jester is dressed more demurely and assists her companion in the comical acting and masquerading. Another character steps into the dance, dressed in buffalo-hide, sporting corn stalks for horns, and he prances in and out of the dancers; this man pretends he is a bull, and symbolizes the evil in nature. At a predetermined signal, an interesting pantomime takes place: the dancers stop solemnly, while one of the clowns attacks the bull, and after a difficult skirmish, the clown finally kills the bull with his whip, and the bull rolls over dead, all to the hilarious amusement of the spectators.

But the character that dominates the scene of *Los Matachines* is the little queen, *la Reina*, who signifies innocence, and she is suitably dressed up as a beautiful bride in white finery. The king is represented by Montezuma, the Aztec ruler of centuries ago. With her fine dancing and acting, the queen becomes the center of attraction, and she twirls and dances between the clowns, the *abuelo* and *abuela,* in lively and graceful rhythmic step.

The haunting momentum of the dance, the pad, pad of stamping Indian feet, the chanting of the chorus and the lively rattling of the children's gourds, all this converges with the shimmering gleam of the many fires and torches to provide a mysterious halo around the statue of the Madonna. The faces of the canopy bearers shine like gleaming bronze, and the fragrant incense of the burning cedar and piñon wood fills the nostrils of everyone, dancers and onlookers. On finishing the ritualistic dance the participants and congregation enter the mission chapel, escorting the Madonna to her place of honor in the church. The *luminarias* or *hogueras* on rooftop and on the snow-swept *plaza* burn gradually into glowing embers as the Indians of Taos slowly climb their ladders, sleepy and cold, but renewed once again in the spirit of Christmas.

And in sharp contrast to the dance of *Los Matachines* at Taos Pueblo, or at other Indian villages, are the fascinating and colorful animal dances. The Pueblo of San Felipe, the Keres-speaking Indian town on the west bank of the Rio Grande, usually presents a series of animal dances in the venerable confines of the mission church. Immediately after *la Misa del Gallo,* after the liturgical services are over, the center of the nave is cleared for the pantomimic animal dances.

The drums come closer and closer to the church, and in come the dancers, received with the joyful whistling and chirping of many young boys who try to imitate a thousand birds. One of the most colorful and entertaining of the animal dances is the Deer Dance, a performance that represents the age-old apology to Almighty God for the Indian necessity of having to hunt many deer every year for winter food. Another favorite dance is the Buffalo Dance, where the dancers naked above the waist and wearing shaggy heads of buffalo or headdresses made to imitate the great beasts, in slow and lumbering melody and step, portray the dangerous hunt for the *cíbolo,* the buffalo that is no longer around.

To keep the spectators from interfering with the animal dances, the San Félipe *puebleños* have devised a group of *caballitos,* several lively Indians who act as a sort of buffer between the participants and the spectators. Simply dressed as horsemen, with a horse's head in front and a funny tail in back, they prance around the dancers trying to be useful, and if a spectator gets too close, the horsemen push him back gently. Other pueblos have the same thing; for example, at Taos, the fun-makers are to be seen at almost every ceremonial or *fiesta,* and there they are called *chifonetes.* But no matter what they are called, or how they are costumed, no matter how funny or outlandish they are, they perform valuable service to the dancers who need to be engrossed in prayerful dancing worship.

Santo Domingo Pueblo, considered one of the Indian villages which has kept its ancient traditions and rituals most purely, puts on not one day of dancing for Christmas but four days. On the 24th of December, *la Noche Buena,* the little children dance, and its basic significance lies in the fact that it is a dance of instruction for the youngsters. On Christmas Day the older children are permitted to show what they can do, to demonstrate how well they've learned from their elders. On the following day the dancing is left up to the young unmarried men, while the fourth day is the dancing for all grown-ups.

San Juan Pueblo is the village in which to see and enjoy the *Tsah-ve-vohs,* those ancient legendary mythological devourers of children. These 'bogey men' come yearly to the pueblo to chastise and then eat up children who have been bad. And the youngsters know that sometimes the only person who can save them, if they've been bad, is their mother who has to buy or redeem them with delicious loaves of bread. The *Tsah-ve-yohs* arrive at the *pueblo,* so the children are told, a week before Christmas, so that any and all bad children can be disciplined, if necessary.

The day after Christmas the *Tsah-ve-yohs* prepare to leave with the helpful assistance of the lively *Koshares,* the black and white striped clowns who represent the spirits of the ancestors, or departed. The *Koshares* and the *Tsah-ve-yohs* have no language problem, and one group depends on the other for specific instructions in the day's festivities and dancing. The *Koshares,* to whom nothing is too sacred to make sport of in their clownish characterization, have a serious duty to perform for the *Tsah-ve-vohs*: they go from house to house in the pueblo to beg food for the 'devourers of bad children,' for their long journey to the Katchina world.

In some pueblos, the colorfully-costumed Eagle Dance is a Christmas specialty, with realistic wing-flying imitation to rhythmical padded-mocassined feet keeping perfect time to the beating of Indian drums. But whatever is one's particular choice of *pueblo* scene or dance performed, all visitors are welcomed at any of the *pueblos* with unfeigned hospitality. The Indians, like the Spanish-speaking *nativos* are happy to share a cultural heritage that is their treasure.

Merry Christmas Amigos

(Pan-American Style)

'Tis the night before Christmas, and
All thru the *casa*
Not a creature is stirring. *¡Caramba!*
¿Qué pasa?
The stockings are hanging *con mucho cuidado*
In hopes that Saint Nicolás will feel *obligado*
To leave a few *cosas aquí* and *allá*
For *chico y chica* (*y* something for me).
Los niños are snuggled all safe in their *camas*
(Some in *vestidos* and some in pajamas)
Their little *cabezas* are full of good things
They're all *esperando lo que* Santa will bring.
But Santa *está* at the corner saloon,
Muy borracho since mid-afternoon.
Mamá is sitting beside *la* big *ventana,*
Shining her rolling pin *para mañana,*
When Santa returns to his home zigzaguiando,
Lit up like the Star Spangled Banner, *cantando;*
And mamá will send him to bed *con a* right
Merry Christmas *a todos, y a todos* good night!

—Anonymous

CHAPTER 10

Viva la Piñata!

Christmas just wouldn't be *la Navidad* — Christ's Birthday — without a *piñata!* It's the annual fiesta-season, and you just couldn't have a successful party without the 'breaking of a *piñata.*' As they say down south of the border, everybody in Mexico makes, breaks, or has something to do with the *piñata* throughout the prescribed nine days of pre-Christmas fiesta making. The season of the colorful *Posadas* — the Seeking of Shelter by Mary and Joseph — is also the best time for a *piñata* party. These two celebrations go hand in hand.

The Italians being a happy and cheerful people, claim that like everything else that's any fun, *piñatas* would seem to have been dreamed up by the *italianos* during the renaissance. ¿Quién sabe? *Piñatas* apparently evolved from a simple pot which was suspended from the ceiling at masquerade balls in Italy. *Pignatta* is what the merry Italians called it, and during the course of the light-hearted festivities, the handsomely decorated clay pot was broken, and its varied contents spilled out for all to share.

But despite the simple fact that the Italians might have invented the *piñata* and that the Spaniards took up the custom with alacrity, it is in Old Mexico that it has become a national art. Among the poorer classes, as still is the custom in both Spain and in Mexico, the *piñata* has a definite purpose: to provide children with small, less expensive gifts on Christmas, since the most important gift-giving day is delayed until the feast of the Epiphany, January 6th. And satisfied with lots of little gifts, *los niños* don't mind waiting for *la fiesta de los Reyes Magos* for the inevitable 'big' gifts. Besides, the Three Magi Kings can't be expected to present the more elaborate gifts stuffed into an ordinary-sized *piñata!*

When it's *piñata* time — and this is not necessarily reserved for Christmas, by any means — a child's best friend is whatever animal he helps to fill with the goodies that will later on fill him. And the *animal favorito* of the Mexican *niño* can and does vary from fiesta to fiesta. One time it might be the patient little *burrito,* or the majestic national symbol the eagle, or it might be an *elefantito* or a pet rooster, or a papier-mache *piñata* that resembles a little boy's dog, or any one of many different kinds of birds and animals that are made up for selling.

Anyone who has ever visited Old Mexico during the Christmas season, especially the last few days before *la Noche Buena,* can walk down the breadth and length of any *mercado,* and be amazed at the fantastic array of colorful *piñatas,* of all colors, shapes and sizes, and, of course, of all prices! In Querétaro, Zacatecas, Toluca and Cuernavaca, for example, there are literally streets full of *piñatas,* thousands of these beautiful decorated clay pots, in all kinds of handsome shapes, hung up on wire, for all to see and buy. Hundreds of children accompany parents, and while papas and mamas haggle over the prices, *los niños* pick one up and then another, until someone decides which *piñata* is going home with them.

During the Christmas season, for the *fiestecita* after the traditional *Posadas,* everybody is ready for the breaking of the *piñata.* And it's guaranteed to crack wide open the sternest and most dignified of facades. And depending upon the ages of the happy participants, the *fiesta* continues until the last *huésped* (invited guest) is partied out.

Little by little — or as the Spanish say *poco a poco* — the piñata habit is being widely, wisely and wildly adopted throughout the United States and the other four parts of the world! Many Americans are held back from enjoying the *piñata-fiestas* because they labor under the delusion that *piñatas* are hard to make. The basic *piñata* is a clay pot covered by colored paper and filled with all kinds of candy, toys, confetti, party favors, or whatever the hostess feels like using. The size can vary, from the pinto bean to large-sized oranges or apples. And the greater the variety of the 'stuffing' the more the kids enjoy it.

Once the *piñata* is stuffed with the goodies and the surprises or the booby prizes, it is ready for hanging. Suspended from a rope from the ceiling, the most important thing is to select a good *piñata* manager, one that can manipulate the *piñata* until the time is ripe for the breaking. At the invitation of the hostess, the participants gather around the suspended *piñata,* and a few of the guests are given the chance to break the *piñata* — blindfolded, of course.

Finally, and usually at discretion of the *piñata* manipulator, if he can hoodwink the person who is swinging the stick or the baseball bat, he arranges for the climax of the game: the *piñata* is broken into a thousand pieces, and the crowd becomes a madhouse. Children, especially, enjoy the monkey-pile, and the more alert come up with hands full of all kinds of goodies. And, in the event that the smaller *niños* come out of the monkey-pile with all too few pieces of candy or gifts, the hostess has a large store of bags full of the items that were stuffed in the broken *piñata.* These extra bags of goodies serve to quiet any disappointments, and the festivities can go on from there without any mishap.

In some of the grade schools in Santa Fe, especially in those classes which are a part of the Spanish Program in the elementary level, 'the *piñata* parties' are held on the last day of school before the Christmas vacation. These children are taught what a *piñata* is, how it's made, what can be put into the *piñata,* and then they decide what they would like for their stuffing of the *piñata.* And everyone enjoys the *fiesta!*

Christmas In Madrid

Heart, I should like so very much to go
Through winter's solemn requiem of snow
With other pilgrims, who from street and lane,
Will travel far to see Madrid again.

This hallowed Eve, born of stark tragedy,
Yet year on year, a blessed memory
For those who stayed behind and kept the lights
Of love aglow, through all these Christmas nights.

Tread softly, heart, amid the seeking throng
Of worshippers, who need no blatant song
Or weird old tale of ancient revelry,
But just a Child, a Star, a lighted tree.

To lead them out from days of fret and shame,
Up winding paths to bright Madrid again,
Where angel hosts appear against the sky
And carols drift on chill winds passing by.

It's midnight, heart, and through the vales and dells,
The padres send the hymns of mission bells;
Kneel here, oh heart, close to the little stall,
Among the Wise Men, Shepherds, Lambs and all

Who need His precious smile to carry on,
Not just for now, but when all this is gone;
When Star and Sheep and Creche are stored away
Until another Eve; heart, let us pray

That God will bless this mountain Bethlehem,
Made through long hours by loving hands of men
Who yearly keep the Light of Christ unfurled
Across a restless, watchful, waiting world.

Come, heart, we go back through the lane
That leads to home and firelight again,
Where you will keep within your archives hid,
Sweet retrospects of Christmas in Madrid.

—Karen Elba (Dec. 1942)

(Reprinted courtesy New Mexico Magazine)

CHAPTER 11

La Cuidad de Belen

The City of Bethlehem

The name Madrid evokes many historical mental images to the *neomejicanos*: it reminds us of Felipe Segundo, that indefatigable ruler of a world-wide empire, the Spanish monarch who deserved the title 'the Prudent King'; Carlos Segundo, during whose reign 'the ancient Kingdom of New Mexico' and its *Villa Real de Santa Fe* was established definitively; and then the noble capital city of Spain brings forth the memory of the great *Reconquistador,* Don Diego de Vargas, Governor and Captain General. But at Christmastime the name of the local ghost-town, Madrid, is nostalgically remembered. For several decades, not too long ago, the village of Madrid and the spirit of *la Navidad* were inseparable.

Every year now several cities in the United States are honored with the distinction of being 'All-American,' for their great enthusiasm in civic-mindedness. Well, way back in 1924, the diminutive coal-mining town of Madrid began a civic program that was to delight thousands upon thousands for many years. And this program had the 'spirit of Christmas' as its theme.

A group of the coal-miners got together one December, a few weeks before Christmas, and they decided to beautify Madrid in preparation of *la Noche Buena*. This grass-roots committee convinced their neighbors and fellow-workers, and even their employers, and soon there were over 400 people involved in the Christmas decoration of little Madrid. An Employees' Club was well organized, and every member donated a certain sum, depending on his salary as a bread-winner. No matter how little or how much each man could afford, the important thing was 'contributing' to the common decoration-fund.

There was nothing more contagious in Madrid than in the Employees' Club's determination to start slowly but surely. The fun of Christmas decorating began at home. A few employees put up trees in their front yards, illuminating them with strings of colored lights. Soon other neighbors decided to spruce up their yards and homes, and each succeeding year the enthusiasm waxed stronger. Decorating their humble homes, the miners soon realized that their meager efforts had brought them much encouraging praise, and if the decorations were skimpy one year, they would do much better the next. And so it grew, until the entire village of Madrid became a showplace.

Once the entire town backed up this unique Christmas decorating program, the Employees' Club was large enough to tackle ambitious projects that would enhance the private decorations. Eventually the miners agreed to donate, per employee, $1.25, and the responsibility of acquiring a twelve to fifteen foot Christmas tree, bringing the suitable evergreen from the nearby Glorieta mountains, stringing it up with sufficient colored lights, and then removing it after the holiday season.

Annually, come December 15th, or the Sunday preceding the middle of the month, between 250 and 300 men could be seen busily engaged in putting up the countless trees, setting up the lights, arranging the numerous biblical displays on the mountainsides, and cleaning up yards and streets and public places. Many of the miners felt it was their responsibility not to shirk the labor, arranging to work on some particular project after their daily shift at the mines. The morale of the employees was never higher than during this day of final decorations. No matter how difficult the job was, or how time-consuming a particular display might prove, happy busy men could be found all over Madrid, each doing his share of the Christmas decorating.

On *la Noche Buena*, the City of Bethlehem, as Madrid came to be called appreciatively, the small mining town was fully astir, and everyone dressed up in his best. What with 50,000 colored lights shining and illuminating in myriad colors every section of the town, countless children wide-eyed and singing Christmas carols at the major displays, adult visiting and congratulating their neighbors on the magnificent decorations, Christmas Eve was an unforgettable night in little Madrid!

Madrid truly deserved the name the City of Bethlehem, for the main theme of the village-wide decorations was the Birth of Christ. Realistic nativity scenes were recreated, and spotlights strategically placed emphasized the rustic scenes of the crèche. Above the manger, on a hillside could be seen huge scenes depicting the apparition of the Angel to the astonished shepherds of Bethlehem, while below this display, yet another project outlined several shepherds on their way to the manger-cave. On an opposite hillock, the Wise Men on camels could be seen making their way down the hill. From a loud-speaker, a voice came over the frosty air singing the traditional yuletide carol "Silent Night, Holy Night." With a reverence that emanated from serious preparation, the villagers came out to the biblical scenes to listen and to absorb ever more deeply the spirit of Christmas.

And since Christmas is the birthday of the Christ Child and consequently the greatest feast day for all children, the Employees' Club always prepared well for the occasion. A special visit from Santa to Madrid was planned; and at the school house, the *niños* delighted in an elaborate display that featured old Saint Nick driving a spirited team of handsome reindeer bounding over the housetops. Music of many sleigh-bells added to the realism of the beneficent Santa Claus.

During the holiday season, the *Madrileños* enjoyed the Christmas spirit to the fullest. There was fun for everybody. Singing of carols, games at the community playground, distribution of gifts to both children and adults, friendly neighborly visiting, attendance at free picture shows, spirited games of shinny on Christmas afternoon, escorting thousands of interested visitors, all this was the direct result of well-organized planning and enthusiasm in their Christmas program.

Fortunately for New Mexico the Christmas spirit of Madrid is certainly not dead nor forgotten, even though the coal-mining town is now almost deserted. Raton, New Mexico, whether consciously or not, has succeeded to the enviable title of *la Ciudad de Belén*. The spirit that once united and uplifted the hearts of the *Madrileños* for well over three decades, now seems to be permeating the citizens of modern Raton.

Through the efforts of an ambitious Raton Lions Club, in 1946, a small Nativity scene was constructed and arranged on the city's Court House lawn. The people of Raton enjoyed this créche-display so much that the following year, 1947, the Lions Club decided on a larger project, but this time the scene was transferred to Climax Canyon. Better lighting and more work went into this project, and the people enjoyed it all the more. The enthusiasm of the Lions Club became contagious throughout the town.

In 1948 the Lions Club conducted a drive for funds among interested businessmen and civic-minded residents, and more elaborate displays were planned. Christmas music was channeled over Climax Canyon by means of well-placed loudspeakers. And so year after year these displays grew in beauty, in size, in design, in popular approval, and more importantly in civic interest. A two year run to a new location along the "old pass" road, where more scenes were added, proved enlightening: the unsuitability of the old road pass in severe Christmas winter weather forced the Lions Club to reconsider going back to Climax Canyon, to everyone's delight.

Today, and we hope for many years to come, Raton deserves the title of the City of Bethlehem for it is a worthy successor to the heartwarming beauty that little Madrid portrayed for so long. Raton can now boast of eighteen different sequence sets, located again in Climax Canyon, where permanent steel mountings were installed for the magnificent Christmas displays. The goal is bettering the ambitious program, for the mutual benefit and enjoyment of the citizens of Raton and the countless visitors who manage to drop in during the holiday season. Raton being on Highways 85-87 and 64, affords many motorists the enviable privilege of enjoying the unique City of

Bethlehem.

Much like the villagers of Madrid, Raton manages to light up the annual Christmas displays around the 15th of December. Many people, even from neighboring states, visit the "City" during the day, yet the displays are ever more impressive and realistic if seen at night, when the magic of well-planned lighting gives life to the many scenes, and appropriate yuletide music stirs the heart to the spirit of Christmas.

For the children's enjoyment, the Lions Club has delightfully arranged a group of story book characters that would entrance the *niños,* the kiddies can thrill to life-size displays of Santa Claus and his wonderful reindeer, ably led by Rudolph, or laugh at the scene portraying Hey Diddle Diddle, the Old Woman in the Shoe, and many other characters that belong to childhood days.

The spirit of Christmas is greatly enhanced by the Raton *Ciudad de Belén,* for the real meaning of the yuletide season is effectively displayed. The colorful and realistic biblical scenes of the Gospel story of Christ's birth in Bethlehem is reverently portrayed, and renews again most forcibly the celestial message of the Angel: "Glory to God in the highest, and on earth, peace to men of good will."

At Christmas

"Man is ever in a struggle and he's oft misunderstood:
 There are days the worst that's in him is the master
  of the good,
 But at Christmas kindness rules him and he puts
  himself aside.
 And his petty hates are vanquished and his heart is
  open wide.
 Oh, I don't know how to say it, but somehow it seems to me,
 That at Christmas man is almost what God sent him
  here to be."

—Edgar A. Guest

EPILOGUE

Recapitulación Breve

Christmas comes but once a year, it is true, but the spirit of *la Noche Buena* permeates and perdures strongly in our lives the year round. It is not only a pious commemoration of Christ's birth, but rather it is a fervent renewal of faith and hope in Almighty God and in our fellow man. It is a challenge to accept the reality of life itself. Just as spring is a promise of summer, and soon enough the leaf-coloring autumn moves in to announce the inevitability of winter, so *la Navidad* prepares us for the rhythm of life the whole year through.

This book has been written, certainly not to impress anyone, but rather to contribute something which is missing in southwestern fast-day living. Ours is an age of progress, in all fields of endeavor, and many times in our zealous attempt to be 'modern,' we miss the trees for the forest. The colorful Indian and Spanish heritage which is a rich legacy to the varifaceted United States can and will disappear if we continue to become ever more indifferent. This generation is young enough to learn, and old enough to know better with regard to the vanishing sense of tradition. Let us save what is worth keeping, carefully eliminating, as it were, the chaff from the wheat.

The sequence of this book is somewhat logical. Respecting the time element involved, the story of each chapter follows through chronologically. December 12th is the great feastday of *la Virgen de Guadalupe*. To anyone who has ever had the honor of visiting the basilica of Tepeyac, on the outskirts of Mexico City, where the *tilma* image of Our Lady of Guadalupe is so devoutly venerated, there can be no denying the haunting simplicity of the fervent piety of the countless pilgrims. To an intelligent Catholic New Mexican—not necessarily a Spanish-speaking devotee—there can be no doubt as to what the fantastic and yet so marvelous apparitions of Our Lady on Tepeyac hill were meant to be to all the Americas. Divine Providence chose a site which would effectively serve as a focal center of the New World. To the north, all the way to present-day Alaska; to the south, through Central America and all through the breadth and length of South America, the Guadalupan message would have a meaning! We have only to read literally the actual words of *la Virgen Guadalupana* to appreciate the transcendental nature of the marvelous apparitions.

"Know and take heed, thou, the least of my sons, that I am Holy Mary, ever Virgin Mother of the true God, for whom we live, the Creator of the world, maker of heaven and earth. I urgently desire that a temple should be built to me here, to bear witness to my love and to my compassion. For I am a merciful Mother to thee and to all thy fellow people in these lands, who love me and trust me and who invoke my help . . ."

And to make doubly sure that the *conquistadores* and the *padres* would have no reason to disqualify the Marian apparitions, Our Lady chose for herself an Arabic-Spanish name: *Guadalupe*. This was a Marian title that inspired great veneration in faraway Spain. Only a few years previously, an intrepid Admiral called Cristóbal Colón had vowed a pilgrimage to the famous medieval shrine of Our Lady of Guadalupe in the land called Estremadura, in central Spain. To the surprised neophyte Juan Diego the beautiful Lady's name probably sounded like *Tequatlaxopeuh* or *Tequatlanopeuh* (she who originated at the summit of the rocks). But Juan's dying uncle, Bernardino, received from Our Lady herself the official title: *Santa María de Guadalupe*.

The Mother of Christ visited Tepeyac hill for a definite reason: to assure both the natives and the *conquistadores* that she was about to 'forge a new country' (for the Mexicans still call Our Lady of Guadalupe, *la Virgen que forjó una patria!*), where both cultures could live side by side in the spirit and love of Jesus Christ. So, when on the eve of December 12th—*la víspera de la fiesta*—we see *luminarias* and *farolitos* burning brightly, we begin to put on, as it were, the joyous Christmas spirit.

The civic-minded *Sociedad Folklórica* in Santa Fe finally took it upon themselves to preserve the fast-disappearing observance of *Las Posadas.* Annually, at historic San Miguel Mission—at what is known as 'the Oldest Church in the United States!'—this tradition-minded feminine group portrays the seeking of shelter by Mary and Joseph. Visitors in the area for the holidays are graciously invited to share in this unique tableau. Not only is the singing and the dialogue between *los peregrinos* (those portraying the Holy Family, on the outside of the church) and *los mesoneros* (those who portray the innkeeper and his family, on the inside) very authentic, but the props are just as good. *Los misterios,* the folk-art images of Mary and Joseph used in Santa Fe are interesting Mexican handicraft, having come up to Santa Fe from that quaint colonial town in the interior of Old Mexico called San Miguel Allende.

The third chapter entitled FAROLITOS ARE NOT LUMINARIAS! is certainly not meant to be controversial, not to create antagonism among southwestern writers who don't know any better. The best reason which I—as a Spanish-speaking *nativo,* a descendant of established New Mexican families—can give for it is an appeal to the truth behind our cherished Christmas traditions. In the spirit of genuine creativity and ever-desirous of promoting what is worthwhile in our indo-hispanic culture, the historic distinctions and explanations were made. Generally speaking, most of our non-Spanish-speaking *amigos* don't mind being corrected when they innocently attempt to enjoy and utilize many of our quaint customs.

Down south of the border, especially in the interior of Old Mexico, in the charming *placitas* and *pueblecitos,* the common people have developed a double-play of good manners and good grammar, which we progressive *Americanos* might do well to emulate. Whenever a *turista* shows enough regard and respect for things Mexican, the tourist will soon find himself being corrected of grammatical errors and idiomatic phrases in his halting attempt to speak their beautiful language. But the Mexican commoner has such a refined and innate sense of dignity and courtesy that it disarms the ordinary visitor, and he soon finds himself learning more and more Spanish. In this same way, perhaps our insistence on the background of many of our Christmas customs will help somewhat to correct so much innocent mis-information, especially in magazine and newspaper interpretations.

The Old Santa Fe Association, still held together by the militant civic-mindedness of venerable Ina Sizer Cassidy, is to be congratulated for their year-round struggle to retain and promote the atmosphere and charm of Old Santa Fe. At Christmas-time the Association sponsors the citywide contest for holiday lighting 'in the old way.' Anyone entering his home in this unique contest of civic beauty has much competition to contend with, so successful has the OSFA been in its Christmas lighting campaign. *Farolitos* shedding their mellow light on adobe roofs, walls and walks; *luminarias,* the burning criss-cross structures of pitch wood; *nacimientos* set up within the houses and yet visible from the outside; all of this forms the important ingredients of the traditional Christmas lighting and decoration.

With regard to the supposedly traditional number of *luminarias* to be lighted on Christmas Eve, let me say that I tried to keep an open mind while doing the necessary research for this book. Despite the simple fact that, as a *latino,* I, too, like to wear my heart on my sleeve, or as the happy-go-lucky Mexicans say *no hay reglas fijas* (there are no fixed rules), permit me to be coldly objective in both Old and New Mexico.

The temperamental urge of the Spanish-speaking people is to be doing something at the first impulse, come Christmas-time and this penchant for *individualidad* comes strongly to the fore. The particular devotion of each person decides on the specific number. For example, someone in a particular neighborhood might feel like preparing and lighting three *luminarias,* one each for Jesus, Mary and Joseph, or for the honor and glory of the Blessed Trinity. Another *vecino* might want to liven up the neighborhood by lighting twelve *lumi-*

narias in front of his home, one for each of the twelve apostles. Still another *compadre* might decide to prepare two tall *luminarias*, extra large, one to honor *el Niño Jesus* and another to repay San Antonio for some extraordinary favor granted him during the past year.

So, to be perfectly honest with my readers, there is no specific number that is required by custom. It is up to the particular devotion of the individual to decide the right number needed. The Spanish-speaking remember with individualistic gusto the old saying: *Cada uno hace lo que le da la gana!* Everybody has the right to do what he thinks best! And in many cases, the availability of suitable wood helps in making a decision; as does the financial means of one's neighbor. What is really *de rigor,* what is really necessary to promote the Christmas spirit all around us, is to prepare at least your first *luminaria* this year; and once you savour the warmth and light of the burning bonfire on *la Noche Buena,* in the festive mood of Christ's coming, permit yourself the treat of lighting up as many *luminarias* as your heart desires, next year. From then on, you won't have any trouble figuring out how many *hogueras,* bonfires, are really necessary.

With *farolitos,* it is the simple matter of the more the merrier. These quaint mellow lights add life to the earth-hugging adobe homes, walls and walks. Ordinary paper sacks are available at practically any food store. There are some stores or shops that specialize in ornamented paper bags. If you are the ingenious festive home decorator, perhaps silhouettes or cut-outs can spruce up some of your *farolitos.* Old die-hard traditionalists insist on un-ornamented paper bags and candles. But being an individualist at heart, I don't mind advocating that you act like the proverbial proud and stubborn Spaniard who insists that *cada castellano en su castillo!* is the best policy. Each man should be the boss in his own home!

Visitors to the City Different—as Santa Fe enjoys to be called—should not miss touring the streets of the town to enjoy the colorful festive lighting of thousands of *farolitos* and countless *luminarias* in their primitive simplicity. Usually the local newspaper will announce the specific homes which have been entered in the lighting contests. The Old Santa Fe Association sends its panel of judges to different sections of Santa Fe at specific hours on Christmas Eve. The Power and Light Company and the NEW MEXICAN also sponsor a contest of electrical lighting and/or a combination of both the traditional and modern lighting methods. And they, too, announce the route to be observed by their panel of judges. Handsome money awards are bestowed on the winners of the various festive lighting contests, which rewards have proven to be an incentive for more and better Christmas lighting in all parts of Santa Fe.

Lightly falling snow, covering everything in sight with a soft mantle of white, burning *luminarias* and mellow-light *farolitos*, all this is the best possible prelude to *la Misa del Gallo*, the Midnight services in the Catholic churches and chapels on *la Noche Buena*. Many people have compared Santa Fe and the surrounding villages and countryside to biblical Palestine. Undoubtedly the warm adobe architecture, the peace and quiet that settles over the land on Christmas Eve, all tend to strengthen the comparison between Santa Fe and the land where Christ was born. But whatever charm our ancient town has, on this Night of Nights, everyone is most welcome to divine services in the Catholic churches. The Midnight Masses throughout the city beckon all devout worshippers, urging everyone to renew again their faith in the fruitful coming of the long-awaited Messiah.

A few years ago many *nativos*, especially our grandparents' generation feared that *Los Pastores*, as a Christmas custom, would soon disappear. Only here and there in scattered *placitas* would some local impresario take the time required to patiently train a troupe in the archaic Spanish of some local version of *El Coloquio de los Pastores*. And these *ensavos*, these long rehearsals often started in early October in order to be ready for the Christmas season. The verbose speeches of the main characters often require extra rehearsals, but still the enthusiasm of the local directors never waned.

I remember how one particular troupe from Rowe, New Mexico, folks who knew my grandparents' family well, came into Santa Fe one Christmas Eve. In those days, some twenty years ago, the troupe would put on their interesting costumes and ride on the back of a large truck through the city, announcing where and when *Los Pastores* would be presented. My grandparents really thought that this was the last time they would ever be presented and so on *la Noche Buena, en la sala de la Unión Protectiva,* a hall at the corner of Acequia Madre and Camino de Monte Sol, we enjoyed for the first time 'The Colloquy of the Shepherds.' This was truly an unforgettable experience!

Fortunately for northern New Mexico there are still some *directores,* who despite the unenviable, thankless hard task of training a troupe, realize that this medieval Christmas drama still has cultural value. I am referring in particular to several teachers of the Española High School, whose renaissance of *Los Pastores* merits them a gold medal for their sincere love for things New Mexican. For several years now, the high school students of Española have enjoyed themselves no end in tackling a difficult dramatic job: that of seriously preparing themselves for a worthwhile production of Old World drama.

What has made the greatest impression on me, as just an interested observer, is not only that the Española High School has dared to attempt to put on *El Coloquio de los Pastores,* but more importantly their attitude toward the dramatic presentation itself, and how they have improved the script. In keeping with tradition the medieval Christmas play was presented entirely in Spanish, and the enthusiastic teacher-directors succeeded in their endeavor to combine the folk elements with the best of modern dramatic techniques.

One bold innovation of this particular troupe was the costuming. Up to then, the local impresario depended on the ingenuity of the troupe itself, and there were no set regulations as to effective costuming. The Española High School troupe compromised between traditional New Mexican folk costumes and modern conceptions of biblical clothing, and the result enhanced the production a hundred-fold. The version used by this young and talented school-group was one which the enthusiastic folklorist Aurora Lucero Lea had compiled and edited many years ago, and the music was based on the work of Alejandro Flores, a well-known old-timer in the native music field.

Up and down Río Arriba and into Santa Fe County, the Española High School troupe traveled to put on their version of *Los Pastores.* Their schedule was one which even professional troupes might have envied. In 1960 they graciously gave of their holiday vacation time and thought nothing of it, permitting their directors to schedule many extra performances. Perhaps their most elaborate and authentic presentations were those that were put on in *El Santuario de Chimayo* and also in the quaint Spanish-colonial atmosphere of the adobe church way up in the high country of Trampas. Both of these presentations were preceded by a candlelight procession into the venerable precincts of these fascinating churches.

Actually, once you have seen any one of the countless versions of *Los Pastores,* you will never feel the same again at Christmas-time. Something in *El Coloquio de los Pastores* will become a part of you from then on. It might be the melody of one of shepherds' lullabies, or some dramatic scene of battle between *San Miguel Arcangel* and the wily Lucifer (the classic battle between GOOD and EVIL) ; or you might remember some stubborn rebuttal from the inordinately lazy Bartolo, or the sage advice from one or other of the shepherds; but there will be something that will take hold of your memory and imagination, and this remembrance will become part of the Christmas spirit, never to be forgotten.

The Southwest in general, and the capital city of Santa Fe in particular, has never forgotten that this 'Land of Enchantment' of ours was aptly called, centuries ago, the 'new Kingdom of St. Francis.' All around us, especially at Christmas time, we can sense and savor and enjoy the spirit of simplicity and the humble but proudly-shouldered poverty that characterized the immortal 'Precursor of the Renaissance,' *San Francisco de Asís,* that cheerful poor man whose saintly earthly life was but an imitation of Christ's.

It is not difficult to imagine way back in 1540, the figure

of that enterprising adventurer-missionary Fray Marcos de Niza trudging over the vast stretches of the Southwest, and then hurrying back to report to the lordly Viceroy Antonio de Mendoza, and later spearheading the magnificent *entrada* of Francisco Vásquez de Coronado; this was only the beginning of the heroic conquest-of-the-spirit of countless Indians by zealous 'sons of St. Francis.' With the resourceful *Adelantado* Don Juan de Oñate came a hardy band of Franciscan *padres,* all of them eager to be sent on official missionary trips to the varied pueblo communities. The first Spanish settlement at *San Juan de los Caballeros* was barely established when the Franciscans were busy at work in the many Indian pueblos, and with extraordinary patience and sincere friendliness they sowed the fertile seeds of Christianity and European civilization.

In the colorful *pueblos* at Christmas-time the spirit of *San Francisco* is quite evident in the yuletide celebration of the nativity of the Christ Child. The simple, but majestic, venerable mission churches serve effectively as authentic manger-scenes for the visual representation of the lowly birth of *el Niño Jesús.* This is an atmosphere which will undoubtedly have gladdened the heart of the man who originated the classic nativity scene in faraway Italian Greccio. And like 'il Poverelo' joyfully singing the Canticle of the Creatures to express his innermost appreciation of 'nature and nature's God,' the pueblo Indians today still continue to dance out their prayerful worship. Complementing the traditional Christian liturgical midnight services—*la Misa del Gallo*—the *puebleños* further add their own indigenous flavor in the colorful and graceful dances of the buffalo, the deer, and the majestic dance of the eagle.

The Christmas spirit reaches its peak in the solemn joyful *Misa de Medianoche,* the midnight services celebrated throughout the snow-carpeted land. And from the historic Cathedral in Santa Fe, just as from countless village chapels and Indian mission churches, the faithful wend their way to happy homes to enjoy and partake of the specially prepared *fiesta* fare. The native New Mexican specialties of the holiday season blend in perfectly with the so-called typical American yuletide foods. *Tamales, enchiladas,* steaming bowls of *posole, sopaipillas, capirotada,* all of these viands, *platillos selectos de fiesta,* emphasize the uniqueness of a southwestern Christmas feastday dinner. An old Mexican toast beautifully describes this holiday feeling: *Salud, pesetas y amor, y mucho tiempo para gozarlas!* Health, money and love, and may God give you a long life to enjoy them!

Visitors to Old Santa Fe inevitably travel around the historic *plaza,* pausing to enjoy the many Christmas decorations and the thousands of *farolitos* that outline the main buildings. La Fonda Hotel 'at the end of the Santa Fe Trail' expresses delightfully the true meaning of the Christmas season with its magnificent outside tableau of St. Francis and the Christ Child, while inside in the peaceful *patio* is displayed a truly distinctive manger scene.

But unfortunately, many of our visitors unconsciously miss *el alma y el corazón de Santa Fe,* that soul and heart which epitomizes the real Christmas spirit of our venerable town. I am referring to *La Conquistadora,* the historic statue of America's oldest Madonna, formally known in English as 'Our Lady of the Conquest.' There in the north chapel of St. Francis Cathedral can be seen the most treasured heirloom of Christianity in the indo-hispanic southwest.

For almost three-and-a-half centuries this historic representation of Christ's Mother has presided over the joys and sorrows, the good days and the bad times, the hopes and tribulations of the people of Santa Fe and New Mexico and of the Southwest. At Christmas-time *La Conquistadora* is regally dressed in colorful gold robes and magnificent crown, and in her hands is placed an ancient *Niño Jesús*—the Christ Child— where from this venerable *santuario* in the Cathedral, the 'Lady Conqueress' exemplifies the ideals and the hopes of Christian New Mexico at its very best. A Christmas visit to Old Santa Fe is not complete without a gracious call on *"La Conquistadora,* Queen and Patroness of the ancient Kingdom of New Mexico and its *Villa* of Santa Fe."

The Christ Child and La Conquistadora

INDEX

SUNSTONE
PRESS

Send for our **free catalog**

and find out more about our books on:

- ❖ The Old West
- ❖ American Indian subjects
- ❖ Western Fiction
- ❖ Architecture
- ❖ Hispanic interest subjects
- ❖ And our line of full-color notecards

Just mail this card or call us on our toll-free number below

_____

Name

_____

Address

_____

City   State   Zip

Send Book Catalog _____   Send Notecard Catalog _____

Sunstone Press / P.O.Box 2321 / Santa Fe, NM 87504
(505) 988-4418   FAX (505) 988-1025   (800)-243-5644